A
Fly Fisher's
Sixty Seasons

Books by Steve Raymond

Fly Fishing—Nonfiction
Kamloops: An Angler's Study of the Kamloops Trout
The Year of the Angler
The Year of the Trout
*Backcasts: A History of the Washington Fly Fishing Club,
1939–1989*
Steelhead Country
The Estuary Flyfisher
Rivers of the Heart: A Fly-Fishing Memoir
Blue Upright: The Flies of a Lifetime
Nervous Water: Variations on a Theme of Fly Fishing
A Fly Fisher's Sixty Seasons: True Tales of Angling Adventures

Fly Fishing—Fiction
Trout Quintet: Five Stories of Life, Liberty, and the Pursuit of Fly Fishing

Civil War History
*In the Very Thickest of the Fight: The Civil War Service of the
78th Illinois Volunteer Infantry Regiment*

A
FLY FISHER'S
SIXTY SEASONS

True Tales of Angling Adventures

STEVE RAYMOND

SKYHORSE PUBLISHING

Skyhorse Publishing books may be purchased in bulk at special discounts for sales promotion, corporate gifts, fund-raising, or educational purposes. Special editions can also be created to specifications. For details, contact the Special Sales Department, Skyhorse Publishing, 307 West 36th Street, 11th Floor, New York, NY 10018 or info@skyhorsepublishing.com.

Skyhorse® and Skyhorse Publishing® are registered trademarks of Skyhorse Publishing, Inc.®, a Delaware corporation.

Visit our website at www.skyhorsepublishing.com.

10 9 8 7 6 5 4 3 2 1

Library of Congress Cataloging-in-Publication Data is available on file.

Cover design by Tom Lau
Cover illustration and part illustrations by Al Hassall

Print ISBN: 978-1-5107-3407-4
Ebook ISBN: 978-1-5107-3408-1

Printed in the United States of America

For Randy
May you have as many seasons

CONTENTS

FIRST CAST

THE TITLE of this book says it all. For sixty years I've been fly fishing and writing about it—ten books before this one—and I'd already been fishing a number of years before I started writing about it. After so many years and so many books, you'd think I'd have said everything I had to say, but it seems there's always something more—some new experience or emergent thought important enough to get down in print while I still have the opportunity.

That's mostly what we have here. That, plus a few old stories published years ago in magazines you probably didn't read, and transcripts of several oral presentations that you probably didn't hear. For good measure, there's even a mostly just-for-fun quiz to gauge your level of fly-fishing sophistication.

The menu includes trout, steelhead, Atlantic salmon, bonefish and, yes, even carp. Also included are rivers, lakes, and salt water. There's a lot about fly-fishing books and writers, fly rods, reels, favorite fishing methods, and guides—some good, others not so much. Just in case you wanted to know, you'll also learn how I survived a thirty-year newspaper career that often interfered with the more important imperative of fly fishing—or vice versa.

A mixed bag, to be sure.

A lot can happen in sixty years, and a lot did. Most of these selections are roughly in chronological order. Some span years or even decades, others the events of only a single day. Some are intended to make you smile, but others are serious, and a few might even make you a little sad. Others, I hope, may inspire you.

That's the menu. Read heartily.

—Steve Raymond

PART I:
EARLY SEASON

"No man is born an angler."—Izaak Walton

"Oh, yeah?"—Steve Raymond

FLY LINES AND BYLINES

IT BEGINS with a fish. I think almost any fish would do, but in my case it was a little trout hooked on a little fly, and I don't think the circumstances could have been any better. From that moment on I wanted nothing more than to spend every day for the rest of my life fly fishing for trout.

That's not an unusual ambition for a boy or even for a grown man (though not usually for a woman at that time). Unfortunately, very few people are ever able to realize it, or even come close. That's because too many things get in the way—the necessity for an education; perhaps a stint of military service, as in my case; the desire to marry and raise a family; the need to make a living; and so on. All those things kept me from fishing every day, or even very often. I managed to fish whenever I could all the way through high school, but then had to put away my tackle for four years of college and two years as a navy officer. The only fishing I had during that time was with my new wife, Joan, during our honeymoon at a remote fishing camp.

Yes, we really did fish.

Then I landed a job as a cub reporter at the *Seattle Times*. Landing a job wasn't the same as landing a trout, but it did give me the wherewithal, and sometimes the opportunity, to resume fishing, which I usually managed to do at least a few days each month.

I also quickly discovered that nothing in my prior experience had quite prepared me for the reality of life at a big-city newspaper. I didn't realize it then, but it was near the end of a colorful era in the history of journalism, a time when newsrooms were inhabited by crusty, hard-drinking, fast-living reporters who sometimes went out and created their own news if none could be found legitimately. The *Times* newsroom still had a few such characters, including reporters like Robert A. Barr, Barney Harvey, and Johnny Reddin.

On my very first day in the newsroom I was seated at a desk directly facing Barr, a feisty little man with a big nose and a rumpled blood-hound face who was already something of a legend in the Seattle newspaper community. I watched in awe as he tried to work a story over the phone. He was a very excitable man who chain-smoked cigarettes and swore about as often as he breathed, and the more excited he got the more he swore and the more he smoked. It wasn't unusual for him to have several cigarettes going at once.

This particular morning, he was chasing a story about a mountain rescue and having trouble getting information. After each fruitless call, he'd slam down the phone, swear, and light another cigarette. I thought I'd heard some major-league profanity in the navy, but Barr was in a class by himself. If he'd been able to write as well as he could swear, he would have won a Pulitzer.

It wasn't long before Barr had five cigarettes going, one in each hand, one stuck behind his ear, one balanced on the edge of his desk, and another in an ashtray. Finally he slammed down the phone again and flipped a cigarette over his shoulder. It landed in a wastebasket full of papers, and you can guess what happened next. Barr sniffed a couple of times, then leaped to his feet and turned to see flames shooting out of the wastebasket. He rushed over and tried to stamp them out, but got his shoe wedged in the wastebasket. So there he was, hopping around on one foot while the other was stuck in this flaming wastebasket and his pants were about to catch fire. About then I began to question my judgment in choosing the *Seattle Times* as a place of employment.

Not for the last time, either. I soon learned that the *Times* was a very conservative institution. The personnel department—what everyone now calls human resources—had only two employees, both former FBI agents, and the records they kept resembled the dossiers of Soviet spies more than employee files. Next door to the publisher's suite was a small office inhabited by a mysterious figure whose job was as much a mystery as he was, although it was rumored he had "something to do with taxes." He was seldom seen outside his office, but once a week he would emerge, stroll through the newsroom without saying a word to anyone, enter the adjoining composing room, and head for the alley, where printers were making up new movie advertisements. There he would closely inspect all the movie ads. If he found any which, in his judgment, contained female images that were not sufficiently clothed, he would take out a black felt-tipped pen and carefully draw additional clothing over their exposed parts, and that's how the ads would appear in the newspaper. This actually happened.

One day he found a printer making up an ad for a movie titled *The Last American Virgin*. He made a beeline for the front office and soon the order came down to change the movie's title in the advertisement. It was published as *The Last American Nice Girl*. Of course the change did not go unnoticed by the public, leaving the *Times* with a huge splotch of egg on its embarrassed face.

Corporate conservatism also pervaded the newsroom. The timber industry, Boeing, and Alaska oil all were sacred cows about which discouraging words were never to appear. When the weather forecast said partly cloudy, it was changed to partly sunny. Individual initiative or enterprise on the part of reporters was tolerated only grudgingly, if at all, and old-timers warned the only way to survive was to "keep your head down in your foxhole, because if you stick it up it might get shot off." That, of course, was not what I wanted to hear, and sometimes I stuck my head up anyway. I suffered a few flesh wounds, but nothing fatal.

Things got better later on—the general liberalization of society eventually forced the newspaper to follow suit—but those early days were very strange, to say the least.

When I got to know Bob Barr a little better, I was surprised to discover that despite his chronic lack of patience, he was a fly fisherman. In fact, he had been fishing near West Yellowstone, Montana, in August 1959 when a great 7.5-magnitude earthquake struck the area, causing widespread destruction and damming the Madison River to create Earthquake Lake. Obeying his newsman's instincts, Barr set aside his fly rods and began phoning the *Times* with daily reports from the earthquake zone, although how he managed it without burning down several telephone booths remains a mystery.

It was no coincidence Barr was in West Yellowstone when the earthquake hit. Disaster followed him around like a faithful old dog. One Fourth of July he obtained a couple of "seal bombs"—explosive devices used by commercial fishermen to frighten seals away from their nets—and set one off on the sidewalk in front of his house. It blew a hole in the sidewalk and sent concrete shrapnel flying in all directions. Several pieces lodged in Barr's legs, sending him to the hospital. While supposedly convalescing in the hospital, he fell out of bed and broke an arm. Things like that happened to Barr all the time.

Despite his propensity for disaster, Barr was popular with other reporters because he was so good at fetching "cabinets." That's what the editors called photographs—"cabinet" photos—of victims of tragedies like fatal car crashes, industrial accidents, or soldiers killed in Vietnam. Reporters were often dispatched to call on bereaved families and ask to borrow a "cabinet" photo for the newspaper to publish. Not surprisingly, most reporters hated these assignments, but Barr was so good at them that most went to him. He had genuine sympathy for the grieving relatives of victims and almost always came away with the desired photo, but that wasn't the end of it. When he returned the image to the suffering family, it was often accompanied by a large floral arrangement, a bag of groceries, or, if Barr thought it was needed, some cash out of his pocket. Beneath his crusty exterior was a proverbial heart of gold, perhaps partly inspired by his own frequent experiences as a victim of misfortune.

Barr and I often talked about fishing together, and against my better judgment I finally accepted his invitation to go fly fishing with him for salmon in Puget Sound. Predictably, the trip ended in multiple disasters. There was a dog with food poisoning (his), the tip section of a brand-new fly rod lost overboard (his again), and a wild, life-threatening ride in a small boat with too little freeboard (also his) through the violent tidal rips and whirlpools of Deception Pass in northern Puget Sound. It didn't bother me that we caught nothing; I felt lucky to escape with my life, and as much as I valued his friendship, I quietly vowed never to risk another fishing trip with Barr.

Which I didn't. But he wasn't the only fly fisher on the *Times* staff. Enos Bradner, who'd been the paper's outdoor editor almost since I was born, had a national reputation as a fly fisher, and we became fast friends. Brad had an encyclopedic knowledge of the state's outdoor history, and during the course of many trips together I acquired a vast fund of knowledge listening to his stories. He also taught me a great deal about the nuances and subtleties of fly fishing, especially for steelhead, and eventually became almost a surrogate father. When he finally got too old to wade rivers, I bought his little fishing cabin on the North Fork of the Stillaguamish River, and I have tried to preserve the cabin exactly as he left it as something of a shrine.

Alan Pratt, the *Times'* zany chief editorial cartoonist, was another ardent fly fisher who became a great friend. His fly-pattern paintings graced my first book, and we made many trips together for steelhead, trout, sea-run cutthroat, and salmon. Al's indefatigable sense of humor made him one of the finest fishing companions anyone could ever wish to have. A fishing trip with him was never dull—as if any fishing trip could ever be dull.

Another fly-fishing newspaperman who became a good friend was Lee Straight, outdoor editor of the *Vancouver Sun*. We fished together several times for steelhead and trout, and Lee's dry sense of humor made him a great companion on the water. I deeply admired his writing, and though he published a number of fishing guides, I always hoped he would write a serious fishing book or two. He never did, but a collection of his newspaper columns is among my valued possessions.

During those early days of my newspaper career it seemed as if something crazy was always happening. One of my favorite stories from that time was told by a reporter who swore he witnessed it while working at the *Tacoma News Tribune*. At that time, long before weather satellites, computers, and Doppler radar, newspapers had to scramble for accurate, up-to-date weather information, and the *News Tribune* had an assistant night city editor whose responsibilities included preparing the daily weather report. He talked the newspaper's management into installing a set of weather instruments on the roof—a rain gauge, temperature recorder, barometric pressure recorder, anemometer—the whole works. Every night he would climb the fire escape with a flashlight, check the instruments, then return downstairs to the newsroom and prepare the weather report.

One rainy night a copy editor got drunk, climbed the fire escape, and urinated in the rain gauge. A little later, when the assistant city editor climbed up to take his readings, it was dark and raining very hard. His flashlight revealed the rain gauge was full to the very brim and he rushed downstairs to write a story that ended up on page one next day. The headline was "Record Rainfall Hits Tacoma."

As a very junior member of the *Times* staff, I had split days off—Thursdays and Sundays. That was fine with me because it was then possible to reach a great deal of fishable water within short driving distance of Seattle, and on Thursdays it was never crowded. There were many small lakes, several well-known steelhead rivers, and a few smaller streams that held trout, and I sampled as many as I could reach in a day's drive, though it was often long after dark when I got home. Some of these waters became favorites, and I returned to them often.

After several months working in the *Times* newsroom, I was assigned to the police beat, where most young reporters were sent for seasoning in those days. I spent more than a year covering that beat, working out of police headquarters, but I also logged plenty of time in hospital emergency rooms, morgues, jails (just visiting), and courtrooms, and saw more dead bodies than I care to remember. I interviewed a woman who had just thrown her baby off a bridge and covered a ship fire on a December morning so cold the ink froze in my pen. I was threatened, shot at, offered (and refused) bribes, and I testified at a murder trial. I interviewed people from every level of society, from hookers and two-bit hoods to the most wealthy and powerful, and met people of every political persuasion, from the head of the American Communist Party to the head of the American Nazi Party.

My office at police headquarters, called the "press room," was shared with a reporter from the *Times'* cross-town rival, the *Seattle Post-Intelligencer.* His name was George McDowell, a crusty old character who had covered the police beat so long he literally knew where all the bodies were buried. He also had carved out a second career as a freelance writer of true-crime articles for magazines, and encouraged me to try my hand at freelancing. I'd never thought of doing that, but it seemed a good idea, so I decided to give it a shot. Since fly fishing was my passion, I decided that should be my topic.

Right away I started collecting rejection slips from outdoor magazines, but then I stumbled onto a story I thought was a surefire winner. It was about opening day on what would be the state's first catch-and-release trout water, a good-sized lake not far from the Canadian border. Sea-run cutthroat annually made their way up a stream that flowed from the lake to Puget Sound, and the lake had become populated with cutthroat. Joan and I got there early on opening day and had good fishing for cutthroat mostly in the sixteen- to seventeen-inch class.

Well, to be more accurate, *she* had good fishing while I mostly rowed the boat and took photos of her landing fish. But I wrote the story and sent it off to a brand-new outdoor magazine called *World Rod and Gun,* whose premier edition I had found on a newsstand. The magazine responded with a letter of acceptance and a promise of fifty dollars payment upon publication. I was elated; it was my first freelance sale!

I looked forward eagerly to the magazine's next issue and when it appeared, there was my story and my photos of Joan landing fish, and I felt a great sense of accomplishment. However, as time passed and the promised fifty-dollar check never arrived, I began wondering about the delay. Finally I called the magazine, only to receive a recorded message that its phone had been disconnected. I learned subsequently the magazine had folded after publishing the issue with my story.

That should have been enough to discourage my freelance writing ambitions, but sometimes I'm a slow learner.

Those days on the police beat were exciting, but after a year I was assigned to cover the county's superior courts. That wasn't nearly as exciting, although it had its moments. After two more years I was offered an editor's position, which I accepted. Being an editor wasn't quite as exciting as being a reporter, but it was always intensely interesting, and I still felt the sense of electricity every newsman feels when he becomes one of the first to know something big has happened and it's his job to tell the rest of the world.

The biggest story I ever worked was the 1980 explosion of Mount St. Helens. That one had a very personal impact because I was out fishing when the mountain blew and got caught in the fall of ash. I drove more than eighty miles through total darkness and swirling ash to escape and went straight to the *Times* newsroom, where I stayed almost around the clock for the next week. *Sports Illustrated* published an account of my experience, and a year later the magazine asked me to do a follow-up story. They also sent a photographer, who, like most photographers I've known, was a little crazy. Maybe it was because of the developing fluid they all had to use in those days.

We chartered a small helicopter and took the doors off so the photographer could lean out and take pictures, then flew up to the crater of the volcano. It was too dangerous to land, so the pilot tried to hover but had trouble controlling the helicopter because of all the heat rising from the lava dome in the crater. That, along with the terrific noise of the helicopter, the rush of steam from the lava dome, and the overpowering smell of sulfur, made it a rather memorable experience. But the photographer got his pictures, and when he was finished he put down his cameras, reached into his shirt pocket, and took out a little brown envelope. He opened the envelope, reached out, and sprinkled its contents into the crater.

"What the hell was that?" I hollered.

"Marijuana seed," he shouted back. "Next time this sucker blows, the whole state's gonna get high!"

Mount St. Helens has never had another eruption close to the magnitude of the 1980 blast, but in November 2012 a large majority of the state's citizens voted to legalize the use of recreational marijuana. I couldn't help wondering if maybe it was because of something in the air.

After seventeen years as an editor, I became a manager, which wasn't nearly as much fun, but offered better pay and benefits, which made some longer fishing trips possible. It also presented a whole new set of challenges—complex budgets, labor contracts, purchase agreements, and all sorts of personnel issues. I spent my last decade at the *Times* coping with those things.

I don't think it would have been possible for me to work very long as a reporter, editor, or manager without having some way to relax and unwind, and my way always was to go fishing. Getting away to spend a few hours casting a fly on a lonely lake or steelhead river never failed to do wonders for my blood pressure and outlook on life. Writing about it also helped relieve stress.

Fly fishing has taken me to some magnificent places—the wilderness of Alaska and northern British Columbia, the coral flats of Christmas Island in the Pacific, the River Dee in Scotland, and the Southern Alps of New Zealand, to mention just a few. It has provided some of the best friends and finest moments of my life. In a way it has almost been like a second career, except I have always enjoyed it far too much to think of it in those terms. When I retired after thirty years at the *Times*, it was mainly so I would have more time to fish and write more stories about fly fishing.

You'll find some of them here.

FREEZER BURN

WHEN I was a kid there were no fly-fishing magazines, so I was stuck reading the so-called general circulation outdoor magazines. That meant I had to read selectively because they published few articles about fly fishing, and even those were sandwiched among pieces about fish species I considered well beneath my eleven-year-old angling dignity, caught by methods I considered far beneath anyone's dignity.

Once in a while, though, I'd stumble across a non-fly-fishing article that caught my attention and at least start reading. Articles about ice fishing seemed especially interesting, although I can't now remember any earthly reason why—unless it was fascination with what looked like the most masochistic sport in the universe. I remember photos of grim-looking, hugely overdressed men squatting next to holes drilled in frozen lakes, waiting for their propped-up rods to dip in answer to the pull of a fish. I figured any fish they caught were probably committing suicide so they wouldn't have to suffer in the icy water anymore. No way did it appear anybody was having fun.

I might have felt differently if I'd lived where lakes routinely freeze over in winter. Not that they don't occasionally freeze around here, but never thick enough to walk on, let alone drill holes in. Generally speaking, fly fishers in my neighborhood don't have to worry about ice.

Except on those occasions when we do—like the time I joined a group of angling friends for an outing at a lake that was open to fishing only during winter, when it was usually too cold for intelligent life to venture outdoors.

We camped not far from the lake, parking our rigs or setting up tents around a large cleared space where we laid a campfire. Nearly everyone had brought firewood, so there was plenty of fuel—a good thing, because as soon as the sun went down the temperature plunged like the stock market in 1929. We built a roaring bonfire and everyone gathered around and stood close for the warmth, talking and sipping coffee, or maybe something stronger.

Then Bill Rundall, a beloved member of our crew, stumbled out of the back of a camper and came over to the fire, carrying a bottle in one hand. Bill was a favorite because he nearly always kept us laughing—sometimes intentionally, sometimes otherwise—mainly through an incredible series of misadventures. Bill wasn't a big man, but chairs seemed to have a nasty habit of collapsing under him without provocation. Sometimes his mishaps were much worse, and no laughing matter. Once he parked his truck at the head of his inclined driveway, then walked down to open his garage door. The truck slipped its brakes, rolled down the driveway, and pinned poor Bill to the door, which landed him in the hospital for a couple of weeks. Given that history, it wasn't surprising that when Bill started making his own wine, not many people were anxious to drink it.

On this frigid night, however, the bottle he had in his hand wasn't wine, so when he joined the circle around the fire someone inevitably asked, "What's in the bottle, Bill?"

"It's called 'Old Cornfield,'" he said. "I got it on coupon special at a hardware store. Anybody want some?"

At first there were no takers. Then one hardy (or perhaps fool-hardy) soul held out an empty cup and Bill filled it nearly to the rim. The fellow took a huge swallow and his eyes swelled till they looked like a pair of eggs fried sunny-side-up. Then his cheeks bal-looned outward and he spouted a great stream of Old Cornfield into the fire, which exploded in a mighty sheet of bright blue flame that singed everyone's eyebrows. When we'd all recovered from the shock and concussion, someone started laughing. Soon all of us were, and another link had been forged in the Rundall legend.

The fireworks were the highlight of the evening, which grew steadily colder, and as our supply of wood dwindled and the flames did likewise, people began heading for what they hoped would be the comfort of their overnight accommodations. In my case, that meant a camper, which, under normal circumstances, I'd always found comfortable.

Not that night. The temperature continued to plunge and my usu-ally warm sleeping bag seemed no thicker than onion skin. I piled blankets on top and that helped some, but it felt as if my ears were on the verge of frostbite. I didn't have a stocking cap, so I wrapped a thick towel around my head, burrowed as deeply as possible into my sleeping bag and heap of blankets, and finally managed to get some sleep.

Next morning I awoke and looked out at a world I didn't recognize. Ice was everywhere, cloaking every limb, every blade of grass, every protuberance of any kind, including my truck and camper. An ice fog had descended during the night and pockets of it were still hanging around like mustard gas in every swale or pocket.

After shivering through a cold breakfast, I coaxed my truck to start and piloted it gingerly over slippery tracks to a spot near the shore of the lake we planned to fish. Nobody else was there yet, but through the steam rising from the lake's surface I could see it had frozen all around the edges during the night. The ice appeared thin, though, and I thought I could probably break through it easily in my aluminum pram.

Dressed in so many layers I could hardly move, I donned a pair of thick gloves so my fingers wouldn't freeze to the aluminum gunwales. Awkwardly, I got the boat off the camper and shoved it into the ice, where it broke through with the sharp crack and tinkle of icy shards. Then, without much hope, I went fishing.

Rowing felt good in that frigid atmosphere and I headed for a spot I'd always liked near the far end of the lake. It was a fair distance, and by the time I got there I'd managed enough exercise that my body temperature might have been getting somewhere close to 98.6 degrees. I anchored on the weedy bottom of the lake, got up, worked out line, and made my first cast. When I started retrieving there was curious resistance on the line, which seemed to increase the farther I retrieved. That's when I realized my rod guides were clogged with ice.

There was only one cure for that, so I started thrusting my rod into the lake after every cast, then waited for the ice to melt in the water, which was warmer than the air. It was a pain in the you-know-what, but there was nothing else to do.

That went on for a while until something happened that made me forget all about the cold, the ice, and the inconvenience of dunking my rod: A strong fish suddenly grabbed my fly, its hard pull sending the ice flying out of the rod guides. The trout rocketed twice out of the water, made a long, powerful run, then settled down to fight it out. The battle was a long one, helping generate a little more welcome body heat, but I finally landed the fish. It was a handsome rainbow of about four pounds, so cold it hurt my hands when I released it. A fourteen-incher soon followed, then another big fish, shaped like a cedar block and maybe even heavier than the first.

It went on like that all the way until noon when somebody must have sounded a whistle I didn't hear, because then the action suddenly stopped. The fog, which had been hovering all around, lifted

gradually and the temperature crawled slowly upward from somewhere far below freezing to somewhere in the neighborhood of forty,
which was much more comfortable. Maybe it was too warm for the
trout, though, because, except for a couple of feeble pulls, I had no
more action.

No complaints. I was well satisfied with the day, and on the long
row back I got to thinking again about those old photos of grim-faced
men squatting on their haunches around holes drilled in frozen lakes,
back in Minnesota or Siberia or wherever, waiting for their propped-
up rods to dip, as if that was ever likely to happen.

I felt very glad I wasn't one of them. I'd just come too close for
comfort.

THE WOLCOTT FACTOR

LIKE MOST fly fishers of my generation, I grew up reading the works of Roderick Haig-Brown, Robert Traver, Arnold Gingrich, Lee Wulff, Vince Marinaro, Nick Lyons, and others. But another author, one most people probably never heard of, had a more direct influence on my early fishing life than any other. His name was Ernest E. Wolcott.

Virtually unknown outside the Pacific Northwest, and not very well known within it, Wolcott's two-volume work was my virtual bible as a young angler. The same was true for several of my contemporaries who also discovered Wolcott's opus, which remains one of the most remarkable pair of books I've ever seen—not for the richness of their prose, which is necessarily rather mechanical, but for the enormous magnitude of the information they contained.

Wolcott retired as a navy officer in 1954 and went to work for what was then called the Washington State Department of Game as co-editor of the department's "Game Bulletin." His real interest, though, was the state's water resources, especially its many lakes and ponds, and he spent a lot of his time trying to learn as much about them as he could. That meant traveling to remote areas of the state, climbing its mountains, exploring its valleys and canyons or flying over them, and taking copious notes about every body of water he saw. He also obtained information from a wide variety of other sources, including fishermen. The unique store of knowledge he collected about these waters eventually led to a transfer from the Game Department to what was then called the State Division of Water Resources, where he found his dream job: compiling a massive inventory of the state's nearly 8,000 lakes and ponds.

The first volume, published in 1961 after many years of research, contained descriptions of 3,813 lakes in nineteen western Washington counties. A second edition was published in 1965, and that was the one I bought as soon as it came off the press.

The timing couldn't have been better. Newly home from the navy myself, I was in the process of trying to explore nearly every likely trout lake, pond, or steelhead river within a day's drive of Seattle. With Wolcott's book and a set of detailed county maps, the task immediately became infinitely easier.

Wolcott's 620-page volume had all the information a fisherman needed. There was a separate entry for each water, including its elevation, surface area (in acres), and maximum depth, if known. Most entries also contained a brief description of the lake's inlets and outlets, if any, along with trout-stocking records and reports of trout or other fish species encountered by anglers. Who could have asked for more?

All this information had been painstakingly collected, compiled, organized, and collated by Wolcott and his assistants. This was long before the advent of computers, so each bit of data had to be recorded by hand and then arranged in geographic order. This also was long before navigational satellites or global positioning systems, so Wolcott had to determine the location of each lake or pond using the Public Land Survey System, a cumbersome method dating all the way back to the Northwest Ordinance of 1787. The system relies on surveys describing the location of geographic features by township, range, section, or subsection, and Wolcott had to apply that system to each of the 3,813 bodies body of water in his western Washington inventory, then plot all of them on maps—a staggering feat.

Many of the waters, especially small ponds, also had no names. Wolcott listed these as "unnamed lakes" but still described their locations as best he could by using the township, range, and section method.

That wasn't all. He also gathered black-and-white photographs of 297 lakes and included them in his book, along with bottom contour charts of 205 more—the latter of inestimable value to fly fishers.

The entry for Pass Lake on Fidalgo Island is a good representative example of Wolcott's work. Long one of the state's most popular fly-fishing waters, the lake was listed in section 23 of Township 34 North, Range 1 East of Skagit County at an elevation approximately 130 feet above sea level. Its surface area was reported at 98.6 acres, its maximum surveyed depth at twenty feet, and its use was described as recreation. The entry also contained the information that the lake was six miles south of the town of Anacortes, three-quarters of a mile north of Deception Pass, and drained into Reservation Bay and Rosario Strait. It also reported a portion of the lake "lies in Deception Pass State Park" (the park was later expanded to include the entire lake) and contained rainbow trout.

Most entries didn't contain that much information, but when you consider the number of entries, the incredible scope of Wolcott's work is evident.

Wolcott wasn't finished, though. He went on to publish a second volume with the same information for 4,051 lakes in twenty eastern Washington counties. I doubt any other state has such an exhaustive record of its lakes, ponds, and other impoundments, or any source of information that could be of greater value to anglers.

When I got my copy of Wolcott's first volume, I turned to it eagerly and studied every page, beginning with the counties closest to home. Many lakes Wolcott charted were high in the Cascades and difficult

to reach, although I noted some as possible future backpacking destinations. It was the lowland trout lakes that attracted most of my
attention. They usually opened for fishing in late April and closed in
September or October, and many were within a reasonable day's drive.
I began assigning numbers to the waters that looked most promising
and wrote each number next to the lake's name in the book's index
so I could find it easily in the voluminous text. Then, using Wolcott's
township-range-section method, I found each lake on a map and identified it by the same number. At least I tried to find them; some lakes
or ponds were too small to show on any map I could find, so sometimes I had to be content with charting approximate locations. My
maps rapidly became speckled with numbers.

Then I began checking out the numbered lakes one by one. I never
got to all of them—there were just too many—but I did visit and/or
fish at least several dozen. Sometimes the results were disappointing; some lakes were surrounded by homes and overcrowded with
fishermen, others so acidic or devoid of insect life they would never
produce sizable trout, still others deficient for any number of reasons.
That was no surprise; I'd expected some negative results. But I also
found about a dozen waters that were shallow, rich with insect life,
and sufficiently untrammeled by civilization to be fished comfortably
and profitably, and I returned to most of them, sometimes often. They
provided a wide variety of fishing for several trout species, but I also
found one lake that Wolcott noted had been experimentally stocked
with Chinook salmon. That alone induced me to try it, which I probably would not have done otherwise, and I was rewarded when the
lake yielded a bright salmon weighing several pounds.

Most of the waters I sampled held relatively small trout, but some
had good mayfly hatches and offered welcome opportunities for dry-
fly fishing, which I needed to practice. Others, which became favorites, produced occasional large trout, sometimes as heavy as three or
four pounds, much bigger than one would normally expect to find
almost within sight of skyscrapers.

My copy of Wolcott's opus soon became beat up, dog eared, and filled with penciled marginal notes.

These exploratory trips were always ripe with optimism and the anticipation of discovery. No two waters were alike—not even remotely—and some had unique features. I looked forward to probing their secrets.

Sometimes, though, my optimism and excitement were quickly extinguished. I visited some lakes that had been charted by Wolcott before they were discovered by real-estate "developers"—"property pimps," I called them—who surrounded them with wall-to-wall homes and septic drain fields that leached toxic cargo into the water. Most of these also had little if any public access. If I tried fishing them at all, which was seldom, they usually yielded nothing more than a few barely legal-sized stocked trout, which could be caught only by dodging water skiers or bait fishermen who crowded too close.

On other occasions I found the way blocked by locked gates decorated with no-trespassing signs or other threats, so there was no way to reach the waters beyond. And despite Wolcott's painstaking efforts to pinpoint the location of each body of water and my own efforts to find them on a map, there were some I never did find, even after spending hours bushwhacking through thick woods and heavy brush.

But if some days ended disappointingly—lots of driving and/or hiking without a single cast to show for it—it was the other days I most remember, those when I found solitude, beauty, and exciting fishing on gleaming lakes hidden in deep woods or shaded canyons. Most held trout, but there were a few exceptions. At the end of one greasy dirt road, I came to a brush-cloaked little lake whose surface was dimpled with small rises. At first I thought they were trout, but when I got out on the water I discovered they were bluegills. I'd never caught a bluegill, had never thought I wanted to, but they came to my little dry fly so eagerly I couldn't tear myself away. They were so small I had to set the hook gently to keep from tossing them over my head, but that was a good thing because it forced me to be more careful. I hooked a fish on nearly every cast, and spent an immensely enjoyable afternoon catching and releasing fish not much bigger than a silver dollar. It was fun, but not enough of a challenge to make me want to repeat it, and I never again fished for bluegills.

Another time Wolcott's instructions led to a pond surrounded by bog laurel and lily pads, and when I tried to get close to the water's edge I found myself treading very gingerly on floating islands of peat. If I stood too long in one spot, I'd start to sink, so I had to cast and retrieve quickly, then move to a new spot. It wasn't a very safe or comfortable way to fish, but there were some big spotted cutthroat to be had, which made the effort worthwhile.

On two occasions Wolcott's inventory took me to small waters that apparently had been mill ponds at some point in their history, and I was unprepared to find myself casting into flooded concrete foundations where conveyor belts had once hauled dripping logs out of the water on a final trip to the saw. The bottoms of both ponds were covered with bark chips, which couldn't have been conducive to insect health, so I was surprised to find good-sized cutthroat in each of them. Despite its bark-lined bottom, one pond also had unusually good mayfly and damselfly hatches. I hiked into it several times and always had good fishing, although I never did get fully accustomed to catching trout within the concrete confines of foundation walls.

Even those Wolcott-inspired trips that turned out badly usually yielded something of value. Nearly every jaunt added to my knowledge of the country and its back roads and trails, and in this way I also learned the woods, watersheds, canyons, and coulees of my native state in a way, I suspect, that few others have.

I also learned a lot about fishing, and a few things about myself.

During the time I was exploring the waters listed in Wolcott's works, I was also still striving to become a successful freelance writer. A couple of my articles had been published in fishing magazines, but I was far from establishing a reputation sufficient to become a regular contributor to any of them, so I was always on the lookout for ideas that might lead to stories. One day I was paging through my battered copy of Wolcott's first volume when I came upon three words that almost seemed to leap off the page. It was his entry for Monte Cristo Lake, and I knew instantly I'd found a surefire title for my next article. What fishing magazine editor could possibly resist a story titled "The Trout of Monte Cristo?" All I had to do was visit the lake, catch a few fish, take photos, then write a story to go with the title.

Wolcott said the lake was in Snohomish County, north of Seattle, "sixteen miles southeast from Darrington and two miles north from Barlow Pass" at an elevation of 1,970 feet. It had a surface area of fourteen acres and a reported maximum depth of thirty feet. The South Fork of the Sauk River flowed into one end and out the other, and the lake was reported to contain rainbow, cutthroat, and eastern brook trout. If I could just get there, catch a few trout, and get a few decent photographs, I'd have everything necessary for a story.

I like to try to learn as much as possible about a place before I go there, so I rummaged through the *Seattle Times* newspaper "morgue" (library) and found Monte Cristo Lake was named for its location near Monte Cristo Peak, which also had lent its name to a nearby town. The town sprouted up after an 1889 gold strike that led to the filing of more than 200 claims and the opening of several mines, which yielded deposits of silver and lead as well as gold. A wagon road was built to the area, a railroad soon followed, and within five years Monte Cristo had become a town with more than 1,000 residents.

Then came a series of floods that damaged the railroad. This was followed by news that gold had been discovered in the Klondike, and prospectors and miners began leaving Monte Cristo in droves for what they hoped would be greener—or more golden—pastures. Mining operations ceased in 1907, after which the town struggled vainly to survive as a tourist destination but finally succumbed to become a virtual ghost town. By the time Joan and I went there, it was almost uninhabited.

The lake was a few miles north of the town, just off a road with the grandiose name of "Mountain Loop Highway"—actually a single-lane, deeply rutted dirt road that was closed during winter and carried little traffic the rest of the year. Nevertheless, it got us close enough to the lake so that we could see it. We found no trail or other evidence of access, but it was all downhill from the road and that made it relatively easy to slide a boat down to the lakeshore. When we got there, we saw that the "lake" was really just a wide spot in the South Fork of the Sauk River, and the size Wolcott had reported seemed greatly inflated. Maybe it was based on an estimate made at high water, because the lake didn't seem more than half the fourteen acres Wolcott said it was.

Undaunted, we shoved off in our boat and set out to explore. The day was bright and the water mostly shallow and very clear, so we could see almost everything. The bottom was covered in silt and appeared to offer little in the way of cover for trout, except for some large colonies of thick weed whose tendrils waved in the current flowing through the "lake." We rowed against the current until we were nearly at the upstream end, then dropped anchor and started casting. Our cameras were handy if one of us should hook a fish.

After covering all the water within casting distance without seeing a single fish, we pulled up the anchor, let the current carry us a little farther downstream, then anchored again and resumed casting. Except for the waving strands of weed on the bottom, we saw no movement—no trout, no flies on the water or in the air. We fished with special care around the weeds, since they appeared to be just about the only likely places trout would hold, but we still didn't see any.

We covered the lake methodically until we finally reached the downstream end and ran out of water to fish. In several hours of fishing we had not seen a single trout. If indeed Monte Cristo Lake held the trout Wolcott said it did, they were nowhere in evidence that day.

Getting the boat back up the slope was a lot harder than getting it down, which only added to our fishless frustration. Our cameras were put away without taking a single shot, and along with them I put away my hope for a surefire fishing story.

I've never returned to Monte Cristo Lake. However, I still think "The Trout of Monte Cristo" would make a great title for a fishing story, so I hereby offer the idea free of charge to any aspiring freelance fishing writer. All you have to do is go there and catch a trout or two—if you can find any.

That setback did little to shake my faith and confidence in Wolcott's work—after all, there might have been trout in the lake when he first saw it—and for several years afterward I continued to rely heavily on his two thick volumes to guide my fishing efforts. By then, however, I'd found plenty of fishing venues I liked and had started returning to them regularly, so I no longer felt the need to spend a lot of time or effort trying to find new ones.

I'd also noticed that some of the waters I had begun fishing thanks to Wolcott were beginning to change. We tend to think of lakes and ponds as stable features, but they can change like almost anything else, although it usually happens so slowly it's hardly noticeable during a human lifetime. Sometimes, however, it happens so rapidly the evidence is visible within just a few years. That's especially true of eutrophic lakes, shallow waters so rich with life they produce organic detritus (dead organisms and waste products, etc.) faster than the rate of decay. The surplus gradually fills in the lake, and in extreme cases the lake slowly becomes a marsh, then finally a meadow.

This process usually happens slowly enough to be almost unnoticeable, but if you fish a eutrophic lake repeatedly over a period of decades, as I have several waters, the changes are anything but subtle. I've watched two formerly rich and once-favorite waters shrink to mere shadows of their former size.

Beaver ponds also are subject to rapid change. Some remain for many years, but if the beavers are trapped out or move to a new location, their untended dams wash away sooner or later and the ponds disappear. Just as often, new ponds are created when beavers move into a new area.

Lakes fed by good-sized streams also frequently show evidence of short-term change. This happens when silt washed down by the stream begins to build up an alluvial fan or delta that gradually expands to become part of the landscape, simultaneously reducing the amount of open water in the lake. This process has been especially noticeable at one lake I've fished for many years; the inlet stream has filled so much of the lake that several acres where I once fished are now dry land.

Lakes and ponds are subject to other changes as well. Decades ago the mammoth Columbia Basin Reclamation Project diverted Columbia River water through a series of canals into the formerly dry "channeled scablands" of eastern Washington, literally making the desert bloom with agricultural development. A side effect was to raise the area's water table, which led to the appearance of scores of so-called "seep lakes" in once-dry canyons and coulees. Many of these became highly productive trout waters, but as the Bureau of Reclamation continues fiddling with the plumbing of its great system, some waters have all but dried up while other new ones have been created. It's getting a little hard to keep track.

Then there is the "beaver complex" that afflicts some real-estate "developers" who dig "lakes" so they can build houses around them. Golf courses with artificial "water hazards" are a similar phenomenon. And for as many ponds as have been constructed for these purposes, others have been drained because they got in someone's way.

All these changes have rendered Wolcott's works increasingly out of date, and many waters that were pristine when I began using his books as a guide have now been rendered worthless for fishing.

What's surprising, though, is how much of his work is still relevant. Technology may have provided faster, easier ways of finding lakes, but you still have to know they exist before you can find them, and for that purpose it remains certain there's no better reference than Wolcott's two-volume magnum opus.

A poet he was not, but anglers never had a better guide or friend than Ernest E. Wolcott.

PAIN MANAGEMENT

THE MORNING sun was still behind the ridge beyond the river when I hooked the fish. The fly, a riffle-hitched Purple Peril, had nearly finished its swing near the tail-out of the pool when the fish knifed through the surface, grabbed it with a great splashing rise, and bounded high in the air at the first touch of the hook. It was big and bright, perhaps eight or nine pounds, a large summer steelhead for this river.

I felt the spurt of adrenaline that always comes when a big fish is hooked and tried to follow as it ran downstream over the lip of the pool into a long stretch of choppy water below. I like reels that make lots of noise, and mine was obliging now, issuing a veritable symphony of excited racket.

The fish took all my line and an ample share of the backing while I stumbled in pursuit. I didn't know this section of the river very well, so I was feeling my way like a blind man through the rocks and boulders on the river floor.

When the run finally ended I couldn't tell exactly where the fish had gone, but I knew it was still on because I could feel it shaking its head angrily, each movement telegraphed through the long, taut line

29

and backing. My pursuit had led me into deeper water, so I changed direction and headed toward the rocky beach, still reeling as I went. The steelhead immediately sensed the change and burst out of the water—once, twice, three times—then started another run, longer than the first. I tried again to follow, continuing to reel while simultaneously watching where I placed my feet among the slippery, unfamiliar rocks.

After a long sprint the steelhead finally paused, then halted altogether, though again I couldn't tell exactly where it was. I kept moving downstream, still reeling, until at last I felt the backing splice slide through the stripping guide. It was followed by several turns of line, then several more, and I continued gaining line with every downstream step until I figured I must be getting pretty close to the fish, although I still had no firm idea where it was.

Suddenly the fish exploded out of the water not thirty feet away. At the apex of its leap it turned and seemed to hang in the air for a long moment while it fixed me with a cold, dark eye. Then it disappeared back in the river and took off on the wildest run yet. Line whistled out, the backing splice followed quickly, and the reel's racket rose to a screech.

And then . . . there was nothing. The line went slack, the rod straightened, the reel fell silent, and instantly I felt the hollow feeling that always comes with realization that a fish has been lost. I won't repeat what I said then, not in polite company anyway, but here's a clue: The word had four letters and one was a vowel.

The empty feeling gave way to pain. It started deep in my gut, down where it always does, spreading upward and outward until it seemed to fill my whole being. It wasn't agonizing like the pain of a kidney stone—I've had several of those, so I knew—but it was sharp enough. Of course the pain of a lost fish is psychological, not physical; it's the pain of acute disappointment, the hurt of irreversible loss, but that hardly makes it any easier to bear.

Trying to ignore what I was feeling, I reeled in to see what damage the fish might have done. Surprisingly, my leader was still intact and the fly still attached, but a closer look revealed the size 4 low-water Atlantic salmon hook had been straightened as neatly as if it had been done in a forge.

What would make a fish do that? Could a steelhead have as much adrenaline as a human? What could motivate such a desperate surge of strength in an eight- or nine-pound fish?

Perhaps it was that laser-like look the fish had given me from the top of its last leap. In all its freshwater life and seaward migrations, it had probably never seen anything quite like me—the sudden image of a broad-brimmed hat perched over a pair of dark glasses with a ruddy beard sticking out around the edges, a sight that must have frightened the poor fish beyond measure. Its only thought, if thought it was, had been a mortal urge to get away from that ugly sight as far and as fast as it could—which, it turned out, was fast enough to straighten a size 4 hook.

I marveled at the irony. While the fish was trying with all its might to get away from me, I was trying with all my hope and skill to fight it to the beach, remove the hook, and return it gently to the river. Of course the fish didn't know that, and its fright had obviously greatly exceeded my desire.

Not a flattering conclusion: A steelhead thought I was so ugly it had straightened the hook in its panic-fueled dash to get away.

That all happened hours ago. Since then I'd fished slowly and carefully downstream until now the sun was nearly ready to slip behind the row of cottonwoods and alders guarding the river's western bank. I'd fished every likely place and quite a few that didn't seem very likely. I hadn't seen a sign of fish in any of them, and nothing had come to my fly.

Now I was tired, my feet hurt, and my waders had started leaking. Not for the first time I hoped the people who make waders aren't the same ones who make space suits for astronauts. Before forcing myself to start the long hike back to camp, I decided a little rest was in order, so I looked around, spied an old bleached log on a nearby gravel bar, and sat down on it gratefully.

The river, where it skirted the edge of the bar, seemed nearly as tired as I was. At this point in its passage it was moving sluggishly while its current scrawled cryptic messages on the surface. The messages were in languages I couldn't understand— Korean? Arabic?— and disappeared quickly, only to be replaced by equally alien texts.

The fly I'd used last was stuck in the hook keeper on my rod. Idly, I removed it for a closer look and saw its hackles had been compressed and battered during its long, riffle-hitched progress down the river. That would never do, so I searched a cluttered pocket in my fishing vest, found the tube of dry-fly dope I knew was there, squeezed a little on my finger, and applied it gently to the hackles. The fly looked better, like a woman who's just applied her makeup.

Then I thought again of the fish I'd lost, as I'd done several times already. Once more I tried to figure out what I might have done differently that could have changed the outcome of the fight. Did I have the drag on the reel set too tight? What if I'd held my rod at a different angle during that final wild run? Would anything have made a difference? Maybe there was nothing more I could have done.

Thinking about it made the pain return. It wasn't quite as sharp as before—the passage of time already had eased it a little—but still strong enough to make me hold my breath and wince. More time was needed before it would finally vanish altogether. I knew that from painful experience.

It made me wonder: If Izaak Walton had it right when he said a man can't lose what he never had, then why does it always hurt so much?

ASK THE GUIDE

I HOPE it won't offend anyone if I confess I'd rather not fish with a guide. That's not because I bear them any ill will; most guides I've met have been really nice people. It's mostly because I'd rather do things myself, which necessarily means fishing without a guide.

There are times, however, when it's impossible to fish without a guide. Some fishing venues require them, whether you want one or not—it's the law. Other waters are accessible only if you have a guide to provide transportation. Fortunately, most guides I've had in those situations were friendly and pleasant, even if not all of them knew their business very well.

The first real guide I had was on my first trip to New Zealand, where I had the great good luck to be invited by the New Zealand government as part of a journalist exchange program. My three-week visit wasn't meant to be a fishing trip, however—at least not as far the government was concerned. Government officials had prepared a long list of things they wanted me to see, expecting me to return home and write about them. The itinerary included visits to a pulp mill, a dental school, a dairy farm, a factory where crop-duster airplanes were manufactured, a sheep station, an agricultural college, several tourist attractions, and other sites.

Fortunately, during the pre-trip vetting process, the government discovered I was a fanatical fly fisher, so they left an open weekend in my schedule when I could try fishing at my own expense. They even arranged a guide, an aging, congenial, bandy-legged little fellow named Geoff Sanderson. He'd lost an eardrum in the war—he didn't say which war—and the hearing in his other ear wasn't much better, so I had to communicate with him mostly by shouting.

He had an interesting history. He'd owned mining interests in northern China and was on a fishing vacation in New Zealand when he received a cryptic telegram: "You may consider that everything you had is lost. The Communists moved in last night." With nothing else to do, he decided to stay in New Zealand and continue fishing—why not?—and eventually became a guide. His clients had included such American fly-fishing luminaries as Ted Trueblood and Joe Brooks, so I felt in good company.

I'd just finished reading a book titled *Trout of the Tongariro,* by Tony Jensen, another New Zealand fishing guide. It made the Tongariro River sound so inviting I decided that's where I wanted to fish, but it was such a fine day when I met Sanderson he suggested we try Lake Taupo instead and save the Tongariro for the following day. That sounded reasonable, so I agreed.

We boarded his boat, a small cabin cruiser with an open cockpit in the stern, made to order for trolling but not well suited for fly casting. An enormous outboard motor was mounted on the transom next to what he called his "small" backup motor, an outboard of "only" seventy-five horsepower. The big motor gave us a jarring, tail-rattling ride as we headed out through wind-driven swells onto the huge lake.

The Tongariro flows into the south end of Lake Taupo through a braided, brush-covered delta with several "mouths" and we spent most of the day fishing those—the so-called Blind Mouth, Hook Mouth, and Main Mouth. Sanderson's technique was to locate a rip where the current flowed from one of the mouths, anchor at the edge, then cast into deep water with a high-density, fast-sinking line. That's not my favorite way to fish, but when in Rome, etc., etc.

We'd been fishing only ten minutes when another boat came alongside, piloted by a warden who asked to see our licenses. I displayed the two Taupo-area daily fishing permits I'd purchased for seventy-five cents each and managed to escape arrest. I also noted the contrast to fishing back home, where I've often gone ten *years* or more without having my license checked.

After about three hours fishing, I hooked a good fish off the Blind Mouth and landed a four-pound rainbow. It made one fair run, but was nothing special. Later I landed and released a ten-inch rainbow. That was our bag for the day.

That night it rained very hard and was still raining next morning. The Tongariro was completely blown out of shape, and fishing it was out of the question. Sanderson presented me a bill for $57 in New Zealand currency, or about US$50, for one day of fishing. Since I'd never hired a guide before, didn't really know what to expect, and wasn't carrying very much money, that seemed high. It was probably a good thing the weather had knocked out the fishing; if I'd had to pay for another day I might have run out of money.

Now—more than forty years later—Sanderson's bill seems laughably cheap.

My wife, Joan, arrived to join me after the first two weeks of my tour and we added another week's stay at our own expense. Fortunately, she brought a fresh supply of traveler's cheques, so I was able to hire the second guide of my fishing life—the previously mentioned Tony Jensen. He was much closer to my age than Sanderson, could hear much better, and we hit it off immediately. He already had another client booked for the first day I wanted to fish, but said the other client was an experienced fisherman who wouldn't mind if he split time between the two of us, assuming that was OK with me. It was.

We started on the Tongariro at the famous Major Jones Pool, where Tony told me where to begin fishing, waited until he was satisfied I seemed to know what I was doing, then left to check on his other client. By the time he returned, I had fished my way to the end of the great crescent-shaped pool and landed five splendid rainbow from three to five pounds. "I could tell by the way you started fishing that you didn't really need a guide," Tony said. "That's why I didn't think you'd mind if I left for a while."

I decided Tony was the kind of guide I like.

Next day he took me farther up the river where we found more trout, and I grew more impressed with his intimate knowledge of the Tongariro. In all, we spent six hours together over two days. His bill was $48.

As I was saying, that's my kind of guide.

Thirteen years passed before I fished with another guide. That was when my friend Dave Draheim and I joined nine other anglers for a trip to Christmas Island in the Pacific, still relatively early in its development as a bonefishing destination. Most of us, including Dave and me, had never fished for bonefish.

When we saw the ubiquitous poverty of the people who lived on the island, it was easy for me to set aside my usual suspicion of people who try to make a living from fly fishing. Instead, I felt privileged to pay the local guides because they so obviously needed the money for their families, even though it soon became evident most of them were still in the very early stages of learning to be guides.

Our first day Dave and I bounced around in the back of a small pickup truck as our "guides" drove a maze of potholed dirt roads, splashed through several lagoons, detoured around rusting military wreckage and fallen coconut palms, and finally dropped us at the shore of a lagoon that looked no different from many others we had passed. When we asked where we should begin fishing, one guide pointed vaguely at the water, then curled up in the front seat of the pickup and went to sleep. The other guide crawled in the back of the truck and followed suit. I didn't complain; if I had to have a guide, which I did in this case, I'd rather leave him snoozing in a truck.

I'd heard many tales of how difficult it was to see bonefish, and Dave and I soon confirmed they were all true, but I was glad to find that out for myself instead of having a guide point it out to me. It also didn't take very long for us to learn to see the fish. After several hours of fishing, and what seemed like several miles of wading, we both got the hang of spotting the ghostlike shadows of cruising bonefish and each of us cast to a dozen or more.

We also learned the truth of something else we'd heard about bonefish—they are extremely wary, and one must be very quiet approaching and casting to them.

I had several follows and two takes for my efforts. One fish slipped the hook and I missed the other. My only catch was a small yellow snapper. Dave, however, landed two bonefish, one a magnificent six-pounder, which would prove to be one of the best of our trip.

On the second day we rode an awkward outboard-powered wooden punt far into the island's main lagoon, where the guides dropped us on a small island, again gestured vaguely at the water, then settled down to snooze under the shelter of the punt's roof. Dark clouds scudded overhead, emitting quick bursts of rain, and only an occasional sun break made it possible to see anything in the water. I cast to one large shadow and hooked what turned out to be a black-tipped reef shark a couple of feet long. Twice it ran deeply into my backing and put up a good fight before I got it in close. Black-tipped reef sharks are aggressive fish, and even a two-footer has a full set of dentures and should not be trifled with, so I cut the leader well above the tippet and let the fish keep the fly.

Later we moved to a pair of what we later learned were called "pancake" flats, large expanses of white coral sand surrounded by deep water. Here we found bonefish coming out of the deep water to feed in shallow channels on the flats, and if we took station on a channel and waited, it was fairly easy to see an incoming fish and cast ahead of it. Despite passing cloud shadows, I hooked eleven bone-fish, broke off one, lost four others, and landed six. The largest was only about two pounds, but it was a lively fish that took out line in high-speed gulps.

Guide assignments were rotated every day through some complex algorithm known only to the chief guide. Some days we were assigned guides we'd had before, other days we weren't. Fishing assignments also were supposedly changed daily to account for tide changes and to assure the same flats weren't fished every day.

That seemed to be the theory, anyway.

One day Dave and I were paired with two other fishermen. After a mediocre, almost fishless morning, we all bounced around in a pickup for nearly an hour until the guides stopped on the shore near a small island. Beyond the island was a flat Dave and I had fished a day earlier, but the guides assured us it would be worth fishing again, then took their accustomed places in the truck and settled down for a nap. We waded a channel to the island, casting to a few bonefish along the way, then crossed the island to the flat on its far side. When we got there, the flat was dry; the tide had already gone out. So we reversed course and returned to the channel we had just crossed, only to find most of the water had drained out of it, too.

By then I'd walked and waded several miles without making more than a few casts. It was two o'clock and the guides announced it was their quitting time. Reluctantly, we got in the truck and plotted revolution while they drove back to the hotel. When we got there, we demanded more fishing time. One guide refused and went home, but the other agreed to take us out again. He took us to a big flat near shore where we fished another couple of hours. There were plenty of bonefish around, but persistent wind and fading late-afternoon light made it almost impossible to see them. Those we did see usually spooked before we could even get a line in the air. I broke off one fish on the strike and lost another that cut my leader on a coral head. It was the most frustrating day of our trip.

Back at the Captain Cook Hotel, I admired a lovely blossom that resembled a large dogwood bloom. Curious to know what it was, I decided to ask the guide. He stared at the blossom, pondered the matter, then gave his answer: "Tropical Flower."

One further bit of evidence of the guides' inexperience was apparent from a sign posted on the wall of the hotel dining room. It recommended contributions to the staff welfare fund "in lieu of tipping."

That would change radically in years to come.

On the first of what would become three trips to Salmon Brook Camp on the Main Southwest Miramichi in New Brunswick, I knew I'd again be fishing with a guide. Not only was a guide required, but I was a complete stranger to the type of fishing I'd be doing, much of which would be from a canoe. So when I was introduced to Charlie Munn, I was ready to place myself completely in his hands.

It was a good decision. Charlie came from a family with a distinguished history among Miramichi fishing guides and had twenty-six years' experience of his own. Even so, at first I was a little nervous fishing from the front of his canoe while he sat in the rear watching everything I did. I felt a bit like a teenager taking his first driving test. But we soon achieved a level of mutual comfort—well, at least *I* felt comfortable—because Charlie had perhaps the best "bedside manner" of any guide I've met. He never said much, and when he did speak it was usually to suggest that "mebbe it's time we tried a different spot" or "mebbe it's time to head back." He prefaced most of his few pronouncements with the word "mebbe," which framed it as a suggestion, never a command.

Even when I screwed up a cast or did something else wrong, he was never critical. But I soon realized he was always concentrating intently on what I was doing, following the progress of the fly on every cast, and if he didn't like what he saw he would say something like "that fly isn't tracking right. Mebbe I better have a look at it." That was about as close as he ever came to a declarative statement.

And if I hooked a fish and lost it, he would always say something intended to make me feel better—"saved you the trouble of releasing it" or "you had your fun with it." I appreciated the sentiments, even if they didn't really ease the pain of losing a fish.

So we usually fished in comfortable silence, both of us watching the fly as it swept through its quartering downstream course. I fished a floating line so the fly was always in the surface film or just beneath, which usually made it possible to see. Charlie often saw fish before I did. "There's a fish after that fly," he would announce, and in the next moment I'd see and feel the strike.

Salmon Brook Camp has exclusive rights to six pools or "beats" on the river, and Charlie knew every one intimately. He also knew where the salmon would be lying at almost any stage of water. I always felt that if there were any fish in the river, Charlie would be able to find them.

That doesn't mean we were always busy fighting fish. Fishing for Atlantic salmon is similar to steelhead fishing in that it usually takes many casts and a healthy dose of patience just to get a single rise or strike. But the fishing in the Miramichi *was* faster than steelhead fishing, partly because the salmon runs are larger than most of the few remaining good steelhead runs on the Pacific Coast, and partly—or maybe mostly—because Charlie knew where the salmon would be.

I also greatly admired his ability to pole the long, heavy canoe, especially upstream against the current. He would thrust his hand-cut spruce pole into the gravel bottom with a satisfying crunch, apply leverage, lean into the pole with all his strength, and drive the canoe forward in spurts of progress. I wouldn't have wanted to try arm wrestling with him.

In eighteen days of fishing over those three trips, I rose nineteen fish, hooked eight, landed three salmon—largest twelve pounds—and several grilse (salmon that had spent only a single winter at sea and usually weighed three to seven pounds).

Thanks, Charlie.

I returned to Christmas Island on the tenth anniversary of my first trip, this time on a magazine assignment to write a story about what had changed on the island since my first visit. I was traveling alone, but there were more than two dozen other fishermen in camp and I quickly made friends with several.

I was most interested to find out what changes might have taken place with the guides. I recognized some from my first trip and it was soon evident they had learned more about what guides are supposed to do. No longer were they just truck drivers or boatmen who dozed away the afternoons while their clients fished; now they had learned to accompany their clients, wading with them and helping them see fish—most guides were much better at that than the visiting anglers—and suggesting when to change flies and what fly they should try.

A few guides had even learned to tie flies, and their day-to-day exposure to the fishing gave them intimate knowledge of the most effective patterns. Another improvement was that the awkward punts we'd used for transportation ten years earlier had been replaced by giant outriggers, each with a central platform, benches, and a roof for protection from the elements. A steersman ran the outboard from a small compartment in the stern while the senior guide usually rode far up in the bow, using hand signals to direct the steersman. The outriggers handled much better than the punts and also were much better at keeping their passengers dry.

However, the seating arrangement offered an irresistible opportunity to at least one guide who apparently missed the afternoon siestas that had been the norm ten years earlier. I discovered this one afternoon when the outrigger droned monotonously across the lagoon for at least an hour, never changing course and bypassing many fishy-looking flats. It finally dawned on me it also had been a very long time since I'd seen the guide up front give any hand signals to the steersman back aft. That's when I realized the guide had been asleep the whole time, costing us (other clients were aboard, too) at least an hour's fishing time.

The same guide later did something that might have gotten him tarred and feathered had he done it anywhere but Christmas Island. I was fishing without a guide that day and had just hooked a sizable bonefish when the guide came trudging up on my right with a client in tow. He saw I was playing a fish and there was plenty of room for him and his fisherman to go behind me; instead, he led his client directly in front of me and lifted my line off the water so both he and the client could duck under it. I was so startled by this egregious breach of angling etiquette I didn't know what to say. Miraculously, the fish was still on and I finally landed it, but I also made it a point to avoid that particular guide for the remainder of the trip.

I was able to fish alone that day because it was then still permissible to fish without a guide on Christmas Island, just by saying you didn't want one. I'd used a guide the first two or three days until I was satisfied I'd regained my "eyes" well enough to see bonefish and note what progress the guides had made since my initial visit, but after that I opted to fish without one. One of those days turned out to be the greatest day of bonefishing I've ever had, with or without a guide, which only served to reinforce my feeling that, when possible, it's often more productive and more fun to fish alone.

When I wrote my article I gave the guides a mixed report, although it was obvious most of the veteran guides had made substantial progress in a decade.

There was one more sign of "progress:" The sign suggesting "contributions to the staff welfare fund in lieu of tipping" was no longer hanging in the dining room at the Captain Cook Hotel.

More about guides later.

THE LOWDOWN ON LUNDBOM

THERE ARE dozens of lakes scattered around the town of Merritt in southern British Columbia, and although Joan and I had spent several days sampling several of them, we had found only mediocre fishing. The only nearby lake we hadn't tried was named Lundbom. I'd been avoiding it for years because I didn't like the name.

"Lund" and "bom," it seemed to me, were a pair of syllables that just didn't fit together. Instead of blending smoothly, they seemed to crash into one another, like a couple of cars on the freeway. At the time I had no idea where the name came from; I just thought it was ugly, and that's why I'd never visited the lake. I suppose only a newspaper editor could be put off by something like that.

Much later I learned from the British Columbia Geographical Names Office that the lake was named for Angus William Lundbom, sometimes spelled Lundboom, a local magistrate in the 1880s. I suppose it wasn't his fault he had such an awkward name; even spelling it Lundboom didn't seem to help much, in my opinion.

But Lundbom/Lundboom did have one thing in his favor: He was perhaps the area's first true conservationist. Environmentalists and conservationists never have had an easy time in British Columbia, and

Lundbom was no exception. He was deeply concerned about what he considered destructive overgrazing of the area's rich grasslands—so concerned he "went out of his mind," according to one area historian. Eventually he was removed from the community—involuntarily.

In later years I would grow to appreciate the great irony of that.

At the time, however, Lundbom Lake was the closest untried water, and I finally decided to put aside my dislike for its awkward name and check it out. So we followed a pair of ruts through a narrow gap between two hills until we came out on the crest of another hill, this one overlooking a valley filled with water: Lundbom Lake.

The lake was long and fairly narrow, lying almost exactly on an east-west axis. If you stretched your imagination, you might think its shape resembled a human foot—the left one. The shoreline on our right, the lake's south side, rose steeply to a high ridge heavily timbered with pine, fir, and groves of aspen. On the foot's north side, rolling hills climbed gradually to a lower ridge covered with grass and sunflowers. A dirt road followed the north shoreline toward the lake's east end, where a shallow bay marked the foot's big toe. The shoreline at that point was bordered by a high, grassy slope with a fringe of timber on top. It was a beautiful spot, and totally deserted.

From the crest of the hill we could see a pair of greasy ruts leading down to the southwest corner of the lake, evidence that people might have camped or launched boats there. I put the carryall—today it would be called a sport-utility vehicle—in low gear and started cautiously down the hill. There was soft ground at the bottom and deep ruts where previous visitors had spun their wheels trying to get free. I stopped short of the ruts, got out, and walked down to the lakeshore to see what Lundbom Lake's larder might hold in terms of trout food.

Weeds in the shallows were teeming with freshwater shrimp, or scuds, always a good sign. I could also see fair numbers of large water boatmen scooting around; another good sign. On the surface of the lake was the floating wreckage of a late-season flight of winged ants. Normally when you see ants on the surface the trout are rushing to take them, but I saw no rises. Not a good sign.

The absence of rises gave us pause, but eventually we decided to launch our boat—I had a lightweight ten-foot wooden rowboat at the time—and start exploring the lake.

A gentle westerly breeze pushed us along the south side of the lake as we fished. The shoreline dropped off rather quickly into deeper water, not apparently very conducive to fly fishing, and nothing came to our flies. We stuck with it, though, and the breeze gradually took us to the far end of the lake, where we could see a rocky point jutting from the other side. The point was guarded by a line of dead fir trees standing in the water, victims of drowning in the high water of spring. Now their skeletal limbs gestured stiffly over the water near the point.

Suddenly I saw a large fish jump near the point. It was the first sign of trout we had seen, so we rowed toward the spot, dropped anchor, and began casting toward shallow water near shore. Joan's first cast had hardly touched the water when her fly was seized by a strong fish that vaulted into the air and fell back with a heavy splash. Its first leap was followed by several more, coupled with a pair of speedy runs, and after a long fight she landed a beautiful Kamloops trout. It was only about seventeen inches long, but very thick and fat, with silver flanks decorated by a slim ribbon of pink.

That was the beginning of fifteen minutes of wild fishing. When it ended we had each landed two fish, all virtually identical, and missed several others. But the breeze had freshened while we were busy exercising the trout, and now sizable waves were lapping at our boat. The anchor began dragging, and before we could react the wind had blown us right into the area where the trout had been feeding. Naturally they fled, and our fun was over.

It took two hours to row against the wind back to the boat launch.

That was our first visit to Lundbom Lake: September 26, 1968.

We spent the night in Merritt and returned to Lundbom the next day. This time we followed the road along the north shore to the rocky point where we'd caught fish the day before. We'd also noticed evidence that people had camped on the point, leaving several rock fire pits. A few aspen also stood on the point, old trees of unusual size, though several bore the marks of beavers and a couple were already lying on the ground. As before, no other people were in sight, and the empty lake stretched before us.

The day was bright and sunny, although a stiff breeze was blowing, again from the west, but the fishing started fast. During the first half hour I took a trout of about two and a half pounds and another a pound heavier. Then the fishing slowed—actually, it stopped altogether. I fished till early evening with no further success, then retired to a campfire Joan had built on the point. We dined on grilled steak while bats dipped and turned overhead and coyotes howled in the hills.

We spent the night there and awoke to a frosty morning. Anxious to start fishing, I vowed to catch a four-pounder before breakfast. It took only a few minutes to make good on the vow. Fishing close to the point, I hooked a strong fish that ran immediately and put up a long struggle before I brought it to hand. On my pocket scale it registered a quarter-pound short of the five-pound mark, the largest fish I'd caught all season.

From then until midafternoon we enjoyed fishing that was never especially fast but always intensely interesting. I released three more trout between two and three pounds each and lost two others while Joan took a three-pounder and lost another good fish. She also caught and released seven smaller trout casting a nymph from shore. The weather was perfect—warm, bright, and calm—and this being a Saturday, we had company for the first time; four or five other boats were on the lake at one time or another.

The fishing tailed off in late afternoon, but we tried again in the evening when a good rise was in progress, the best we'd seen.

Nothing was visible on the surface, however, and the trout ignored the assortment of dry flies and nymphs we offered.

"This has to rank as one of the better lakes I've seen," I wrote in my diary that evening. "It has a fine gravel bottom, underwater weed beds, plenty of natural feed, and splendid fish. We will have to return to Lundbom."

Even though I still didn't like its name.

We did return, the following June, arriving on what became an unbearably hot day with the temperature in the nineties. The sun was a fiery blot in a glassy sky, but the usual westerly breeze offered comfort. Our daughter, Stephanie, had been born in December and was with us, which meant Joan spent most of her time ashore looking after her while I fished, with pauses for lunch and to spell Joan so she could fish a while. I landed seven trout for my efforts, but the largest weighed only a pound. There was little sign of the bigger fish we had seen in the fall.

But we did see something else remarkable: Traveling sedges were hatching, mostly at the west end of the lake, and they were big, some an inch and a half long. They popped to the surface, spread their wings to dry, then started motoring around in random patterns. Trout can scarcely resist such big, mobile targets, but on this day only smaller trout seemed interested. Two fell for my skated imitation and four others took a sedge pupa imitation I'd tied earlier in the day. Joan landed a dark fish of about three pounds and a smaller fish on a skated Muddler Minnow, and we both missed many other strikes in the windy chop.

The next day also was hot and bright. After fishing briefly in the morning without result, we decided to break camp and spent the remainder of the day and all the next visiting some of the other nearby lakes. After experiencing minimal results, we returned to Lundbom "not because we expected to find any better angling," I wrote, "but because it has become one of our favorite spots and is certainly one of the most attractive places I know."

As usual, we had the lake to ourselves. The absence of other fisher-men seemed mysterious, but we assumed it was because the fishing in Lundbom wasn't very easy and never very fast. Having witnessed many crowded angling venues, I certainly wasn't bothered by the fact that most of the time we seemed to have Lundbom to ourselves. Maybe other people didn't like its name either.

The next day was Friday the thirteenth. The sedges were still hatch-ing and trout were rising, but as before they were mostly small. Eight fell for my imitations, the largest only thirteen inches. Afternoon, however, brought a long-hoped-for change in the weather as a brief thunderstorm gave us a hard shower. A young mule deer buck, his twin spikes still covered in velvet, wandered through our camp on the rocky point, chased by thunder. We fished again in the evening, hop-ing the change in weather might bring bigger fish to the surface, but again only small trout came to our flies.

That was the last day of our trip.

We returned on a warm Indian summer day in late September. I landed eight trout that day, including five weighing more than two pounds each and a couple that weighed three. We had visited several other lakes earlier, but "Lundbom was much more alive than any of the others," I wrote. "It was teeming with shrimp, as usual, and there was a good hatch of water boatmen. Chironomids emerged throughout the day and for a while there were black ants on the water. Fish rose steadily all day . . . A beautiful sunset capped a fine day of fishing."

For the next two days I fished under cloudless autumn skies, with only a gentle riffle on the water, but the bright sun seemed to have put a damper on trout activity. Nevertheless, Joan and I each landed sev-eral fish as large as three pounds and I managed to lose a couple that looked bigger. Most of the trout were feeding on scuds, but a couple had been taking water boatmen.

For us the year 1971 passed without a trip to Lundbom, but on May 25, 1972, I left Joan and Stephanie at a motel in Merritt and drove alone to the lake, arriving in late afternoon. It was a lovely warm spring day and the lake was as pretty as ever. Over the next few hours I hooked six trout on a scud pattern and landed only three, but the smallest weighed four pounds and the largest six and a half. When the sun finally dipped below the horizon, the activity ended, leaving a glass-calm lake with a nearly full moon floating overhead—a scene of beauty to thrill the soul.

It was after 10 p.m. when I got back to the motel in Merritt. Joan was waiting with a message that Roger LeCompte, the motel proprietor, wanted to interview me for his "fishing report" show on CJNL, the local radio station, which was scheduled to air at 7:15 the next morning. He had left word for me to come see him no matter how late the hour.

I'd met Roger previously and knew him as a highly voluble self-styled fishing guide. He'd read my book about Kamloops trout and apparently considered me something of a celebrity, although I hardly felt the part. I was dead tired, but went to his quarters anyway, prepared for an interminable monologue, and that's what I got. Roger discoursed at length on fishing acquaintances, a half-dozen lakes, and local fish-stocking records. Finally he got around to his "broadcast," turned on a tape recorder, and started asking questions and recording my answers, although by then I was so fatigued I hardly knew what I was saying. When the interview was over, he left to deliver the recording to the home of the CJNL morning announcer, and I gratefully headed back to my room.

Joan wanted to know about the interview, but the only thing I could clearly remember from Roger's monologue was his intriguing theory of why Lundbom Lake was so productive. Speaking in a thick French-Canadian accent, which made it sound as if he were talking through his nose, he had said: "In zee fall when zee water iz low, zee cowz goez down to zee shore and shitz. Zen in zee spring, when zee water iz high, it covers up zee shitz and zee lake is fertilized."

I was desperate for sleep, but Joan wanted to hear the radio broadcast and set the alarm clock for 7 a.m. When it went off she got up and turned on CJNL. Waking up to twangy country and western music isn't my idea of a good start to the day, but that's how my day started. We listened in anticipation until it was 7:15, but the music continued without interruption. The same thing happened at 7:30. Finally, about a quarter to 8, the sad songs of lost loves and alcoholic cowboys ended abruptly and an announcer came on. "My apologies to fishermen who were expecting the fishing report at 7:15," he said. "I blew it. Left the darn thing at home."

So much for my radio debut in Merritt.

Maybe it was a good thing; I'd been so tired I didn't remember anything I'd said during the interview. I might even have mentioned Lundbom Lake, and I didn't think it needed any publicity.

That would come soon enough.

WEIGHT FORWARD

THE FIRST time I heard the term "weight forward," I thought they were talking about me. Then I realized the conversation was actually about what was at the time a revolutionary idea in fly-line design, a line thick at one end and thin at the other. That was a radical departure from the double-tapered lines—thick in the middle and thin at both ends—that were then in common use.

The big advantage of a double taper was that when one end wore out, you could reverse the line and continue using the other end, thus saving the cost of a new line—about $6.50, which seemed like a lot of money in those days. The new weight-forward design offered a wholly different advantage: A thick section of line at one end would pull the thinner running line behind it, making longer casts possible. Of course, when the line wore out you'd have to plunk down money for a new one, but that seemed like a minor trade-off. Who wouldn't want to cast farther?

So when the first commercially made weight-forward line came on the market, I quickly bought one and loaded it onto a reel. I couldn't wait to try it out.

The place I chose to do that was a trout-filled lake in the heart of the Columbia Basin, and it took only the first few casts for the new line to prove its worth. It not only cast farther than a double-taper, but casting seemed a lot easier, and I was delighted with the line's performance.

I'd been fishing only a little while when I saw a big trout rise far out. I double-hauled and shot line toward the spot, and right away I could tell this was by far the longest cast I'd ever made. The weight-forward belly of the line flew an incredible distance across the lake, well past my target, and finally fell to the water and sank slowly out of sight.

It was only then I realized the weight-forward section was no longer attached to the rest of the line; the line had come apart in mid-air. Apparently the company that made it hadn't yet quite perfected the process for joining thick and thin sections together. Perhaps it never did, because within a few years the company disappeared, just like the business end of my new line.

Other manufacturers were quick to take its place, however, and over the years they've carried the weight-forward idea to some ridiculous lengths, if you'll pardon the expression. Now the market is saturated with lines made for a variety of specific tasks that once would have seemed unimaginable. There are different tapers tailored specifically for trout, bass, bonefish, tarpon, steelhead, salmon, panfish, pike, muskies, redfish, billfish, striped bass, bluefish, permit, and maybe for some other species I haven't yet seen advertised. There are also tapers made specifically for use with streamers, nymphs, or bass bugs, other lines made expressly for saltwater or stillwater fishing (but not both), still others for use only in warm or cold water (but not both) or for the tropics. And don't forget shooting heads, or the new family of tapers for two-handed or Spey rods.

Most of these lines also come in an exciting variety of designer colors with names like peach, mustard, ice blue, sage, glacial, moss, camo, goldenrod, lime, and buckskin. Next thing you know some manufacturer will come out with lines designed for use only in Standard Time or Daylight Saving Time (but not both). They'll come in colors with names like peanut butter, pomegranate, or dental floss.

Forgive me for being cynical, but I have to wonder whether all these specialized designs, tapers, and colors really serve any useful purposes, or if they are merely the result of clever marketing techniques, or perhaps both. I don't profess to know the answer, but for whatever it's worth, I will say I've had better results on tropical flats with a "bonefish taper" than with a standard, garden-variety weight-forward line. So maybe there's more to all this than mere marketing hype.

But one thing I do know for sure: The explosion in fly-line designs has been accompanied by an explosion in their prices. I paid $8.50 for that first weight-forward line, the one that flew away. It was 105 feet long, which was more or less standard then, and that meant it cost about eight cents a foot. Recently, on a day when the weather was too nasty to go fishing, I spent time comparing the cost of 141 modern fly lines from five different manufacturers and found the average line now costs 69.6 cents a foot—more than eight times what I paid for my first weight-forward line. Many new lines also are less than 105 feet long; if you double-haul one of them, you might find yourself holding onto the backing.

The least expensive line among those sampled was thirty-two cents a foot, but it was an unexciting, non-designer color (brown). Even so, it was nearly four times the price of my first ill-fated weight-forward line (which was a monotonous non-designer green). The most expensive line in the sample cost $2.30 a foot, but it was a twenty-three-foot shooting head. As a rule, I found the shorter the line, the higher the cost per foot. I guess that's not surprising.

Why do these specialized new lines cost so much? Inflation surely has a lot to do with it, and of course there have been great—and sometimes costly—improvements in the quality of fly lines; they don't often come apart in mid-air anymore, for example. Perhaps economies of scale also are no longer possible because of all the different specialized tapers manufacturers are producing. It also probably costs more to make lines in all those exciting designer colors.

So maybe the higher prices are justified. That's especially true if you compare the price of fly lines with some other fishing essentials that are measured by length, such as fly rods, wading-boot laces, cigars, and wader belts.

Consider a nine-foot, 6-weight fly rod. A comparison of prices of forty-one graphite models from six manufacturers (only a small fraction of the total number of nine-foot 6 weights on the market) showed an average cost of $348.59 per rod. That works out to $38.73 a foot.

Replacement laces for your wading boots come in seventy-four-inch lengths and $4.95 seems the standard price, although one tackle catalog sells them for $7.95. That's only eight cents a foot at the former price—reminiscent of my first weight-forward fly line—or thirteen cents at the latter price, still apparently a bargain. Remember, though, these laces are not tapered. And they usually don't come in designer colors.

It almost goes without saying that a well-equipped fly fisherman should always have at least one cigar in his pocket, and you can buy a Cohiba Classic Toro over the internet for an average price of $9.15. The Toro is six inches long, so that works out to $18.30 a foot. The Nub, another popular cigar, is nearly as short as its name; the Nub 460 Connecticut measures just four inches but costs an average of five dollars. That's fifteen dollars a foot—a lot more expensive than a fly line.

As for wader belts, you have a choice of plain old ordinary black or camo colors. The standard price is $3.90 a foot for black and $6.51 a foot for camo. They both come in a standard length of forty-six inches—just about the right size for a weight-forward fly fisherman. But they aren't tapered.

That's how things stand right now, anyway. Prices subject to change without notice.

PART II:
MIDSEASON

*"If I'm not going to catch
anything, I'd rather not catch anything
on flies."*—attributed to Bob Lawless

A SEASONAL PASSION

FIRST IMPRESSIONS are always the most vivid and memorable. So it is, years after the event, I still remember my first summer-run steelhead on the fly as clearly as if I had caught it only moments ago, as if its fresh river scent were still clinging to my hands.

I remember nearly everything about that day: how the air felt warm and gentle after the previous day's rain, how the sky was a hot summer blue and the thick woods were bright with summer foliage. I remember the river, low and clear and friendly in its reduced August flow, its deep-throated winter sound having long since lapsed into a relaxed summer murmur.

I remember the fly, a small dark pattern, and the pleasure of casting a long line that carried it to the far side of the run I had chosen to fish. I remember the run as well, a slice of deep water with large boulders whose dark, amber-gray shapes could be seen dimly beneath the gently rippled surface.

But most of all I remember what happened next: how, after only a few moments of fishing, the drifting fly came suddenly to a hard stop as if stuck fast on a submerged limb; how I lifted the rod cautiously to test the resistance and felt a throbbing surge of strength at the other end; how the line began cutting through the water and peeling swiftly off the reel.

I remember the jump, the glorious sight of a great gleaming fish suddenly, incredibly tumbling through the air end over end like a huge silver football. I can still see it as if it were recorded on a film running in slow motion through my memory, a film I watch often and never grow tired of seeing.

I remember the ebb and flow of the battle that followed and how I finally eased the exhausted fish into shallow water near the shore and knelt down to behold it, and how suddenly it seemed as if all the brightness of the river had somehow transferred itself to the fish, with sunlight sparkling from each individual sculptured silver scale. For me it was a moment of deep feeling, not only because of the beauty of the living treasure at my feet, but because it was the first steelhead I had ever taken without assistance or coaching, and it had been long and hard in coming. My memory of it remains as clear and strong as the instinct that brought the fish halfway across the world to the pool where I caught it.

I also know now what I did not know then: That fish would change my life—indeed, is changing it still.

More than forty years have passed since the August morning of that encounter. Before that day I had never been a confirmed steelhead angler. I had cut my angling teeth on trout and they were still my first love. On winter days I would pass up the crowded steelhead rivers and slip away instead to explore saltwater estuaries for enigmatic sea-run cutthroat; in summer I would head into the mountains to prospect for trout in alpine lakes and ponds, again leaving the steelhead rivers to others.

Young as I was then, I was still preoccupied with the need for angling success, and steelhead fishing seemed a highly uncertain prospect compared with trout fishing of almost any kind. When I fished for steelhead at all—which was not often—I did so with bleak expectations, a prophecy that always proved self-fulfilling. Each time it fulfilled itself I would return to my more faithful and willing trout.

A large part of the difficulty was that I had little idea what I was doing when it came to steelhead fly fishing. I was determined to learn everything myself, without help—a prospect, I now realize, that was both foolish and stubborn.

That approach, combined with an impatience that kept me from spending the time necessary to learn anything meaningful about steelhead, meant that I progressed slowly, if at all, until finally I was taken under the wings of two generous older and much wiser steelhead anglers, Enos Bradner and Ralph Wahl. With their coaching and instruction, I began to learn the things that eventually led to that first summer steelhead on the fly.

That fish, and the others that soon followed, had a profound effect on my angling habits. Summer trout were quickly forgotten; suddenly I had no thought for anything but steelhead. Without realizing it was even happening, I had been seduced by their power and grace. Each time I experienced their wild, primal strength I felt as if I had somehow tapped into one of nature's deepest veins, a vein flowing and throbbing with hidden truths and meanings. It was like a narcotic, and I was becoming an addict.

Summer steelhead became my pastime, my preoccupation, my consuming passion.

And so they are still. But it is strictly a seasonal passion; I have never quite developed the same feeling or affection for winter steelhead that I have for summer-runs. It's not for lack of trying—I fish for winter steelhead whenever weather and circumstances permit—but it is never quite the same as summer fishing, and I do not feel quite the same about it.

In my part of the world the first big runs of winter steelhead usually enter the rivers early in December, and that's when the first big crowds of winter steelhead fishermen head out to fish for them. Sometimes

I go along, searching the crowded rivers for a place where a fly fisherman can practice his sport, but such places are increasingly hard to find near the cities. So instead I often revert to my old estuary habit and spend my winter days exploring the ever-restless tides for schools of cutthroat. Sometimes I find winter steelhead in the estuaries, too, and it is always a welcome treat to come upon them, but their presence is never a sure thing.

Crowded rivers are certainly one reason I have never developed a strong allegiance for winter steelhead fishing. The industrial-strength tactics usually employed to fish the winter runs also are less appealing to me, as is the frequent necessity of exposing one's self to fairly brutal and extreme weather conditions. The weather also limits opportunities; on many winter days the rivers are too high and dirty to think of fishing, a circumstance that probably contributes to the size of the crowds on those days when fishing is possible.

Winter also affords only limited hours of daylight in the northern latitudes where steelhead dwell, so even if other conditions are favorable, an angler can scarcely hope for more than eight or nine hours of fishing time—barely more than half the allowance of a summer day.

All these have something to do with my relative lack of passion for winter steelhead angling. But lest it seem as if I have merely become a fair-weather fisherman in my old age, let me quickly add that I think the truth is not so much that I do not love winter fish, winter rivers, or winter weather; it's just that I love summer fish, summer rivers, and summer weather so much more.

One reason I feel that way is the willingness of summer rivers to reveal so much of themselves. In summer the water is low—most of the time, anyway—and it is possible to see the rocky ribs and vertebrae that give each river its form and shape and substance. I like this because it gives me a chance to know a river on the most intimate terms, to gain an understanding of it that I could never obtain in winter.

Summer also offers the chance to employ lighter tackle and more subtle tactics. Winter steelhead fishing has always seemed to me a contest of brute strength and endurance, with heavy rods, heavy lines, and heavy flies; summer fishing, by contrast, requires finesse—a careful approach, quiet wading, and the use of light tackle, light lines, and small flies. Even more important, summer offers opportunities to use a riffle-hitched dry fly or traditional upstream dry-fly presentation with confidence in the result—something usually lacking in winter fishing.

Sometimes in summer the water is even low and clear enough to reveal a steelhead or two holding cautiously in a well-chosen lie, and that is the best circumstance of all. For me there is nothing more exciting than being able to see and stalk an individual fish, then watch its response as I change flies or tactics, trying to tease the fish even as with its visible presence it teases me. Such opportunities come rarely in winter.

Summer rivers have many other charms. The tracks of birds and small animals in the wet sand along the shores of a river reveal countless fascinating dramas if one takes the time to study and decipher them. Much of interest is also to be gleaned from the tumbled rocks on the river bars. The earth's skeleton is here revealed, with all the topsoil stripped away, and the exposed gravel bars of late summer offer a glimpse of what lies beneath everything but is seldom seen. I find pleasure in studying these things and wonder about the origins of these rocks and whether they came from deep within the earth, spewed up by some hellish volcanic fire, or if they were crushed into hardness by the relentless pressure of some ancient sea.

But there is still more to be seen. Sometimes along the riverside path I will find the telltale sign of a bear that has been raiding a nearby orchard, or a vantage point from which to watch a stately blue heron fish the river shallows with a quiet patience that seems measured in light years. Feisty kingfishers are common, and I love hearing their raucous chatter and watching their darting flight from limb to limb;

I often think that if I were a bird I should want to be a kingfisher and live near rivers.

An osprey sometimes circles overhead in its aerial hunt, and beyond it an eagle cruises at even higher altitude, hoping the osprey will drop its catch. Swift mergansers fly up and down the river like feathered missiles, and the riverside foliage is continually alive with the quick movement and songs of robins, finches, cedar waxwings, and other birds. At twilight the nighthawks and bats swoop down to feed among the hordes of insects rising from the river, and it's amusing to toss pebbles in the air and watch the gullible bats chase after them in sonic confusion.

But of all the sights and sounds along a summer river, I most love watching the homely little water ouzel hop and bob from rock to rock along the river's edge. If I am lucky, the ouzel also will favor me with its extraordinarily sweet song.

All these things form an important part of the attraction of summer steelhead fishing, and they never fail to give me immense satisfaction—but I do not allow them to distract me from the fundamental point and purpose of my presence on the river: I am there to catch steelhead. That remains the basic reason and the goal, the final inducement that draws me to the river like a moth to a flame. When all else is said and done, the ultimate experience of summer steelhead fishing is still to witness the graceful rise of a bright fish to a floating fly, to set the hook, and enjoy the spectacular fight that follows.

I came to summer steelhead fly fishing too late to enjoy the best of it. But I was fortunate to come in time to know some of the generation of anglers who first defined the sport.

Enos Bradner and Ralph Wahl were among them, and no angler could have wished for a better pair of mentors than they were to me. Mostly through them, I was also fortunate enough to meet many others, men like Tommy Brayshaw, Walt Johnson, Frank Headrick, Roderick Haig-Brown, Mike Kennedy, Don Ives, Ken McLeod,

Al Knudson, Wes Drain, Joe Pierce, and Syd Glasso. I learned from all of them, since all had made their own significant contributions to the sport, and some became my fast friends.

Sadly, all are gone now. Gone with them are most of the wild summer steelhead, although surely that was no fault of theirs. The fishermen were victims of old age, the fish victims of logging, dams, industrial and real-estate "development," highway construction, commercial fishing, and all the other evils that men do to fish, best summed up as poor stewardship.

Paradoxically, in the years the wild runs were dwindling, the number of anglers fishing them was increasing exponentially. Now much smaller numbers of fish must be shared among a much larger population of anglers, at least on the heavily fished rivers, and the inevitable result is that each angler catches fewer fish.

This is not a pleasant thing to contemplate, but the consequences have not all been bad. It's a fact of life in angling as well as economics that when demand is up and supply is down, those responsible for generating the demand will find new ways of getting what they want. This has certainly been true of steelhead fly fishers, and it has inspired the development of many new and innovative fishing tactics in recent years, including the growing use of waking flies, upstream nymphs, and the greased-line method. Accompanying these changes have been great new strides in steelhead fly-tying techniques and materials.

These things eventually might have happened anyway, but the decline of summer steelhead runs coupled with the increasing population of anglers has undoubtedly hastened their development; together they represent enormous change from the conventional angling wisdom of a half century ago. Competition has necessarily made more sophisticated anglers of us all.

I think, on an individual level, it also has made us better. Certainly it has made me a more thoughtful and careful fisherman than I used to be. Now I take the time to weigh my approach to every run or riffle, to make each cast with care, and to fish every pocket or patch of water where a steelhead might conceivably hold.

It's hard to measure the results of this. Like most anglers on hard-fished rivers, my rate of angling success is not what it used to be, but it might be even less were it not for these added measures. Perhaps that in itself is a sign of success in an age of fewer steelhead, the most we can hope. But even if I catch nothing, at least now I can leave the river feeling satisfied that I have fished it thoroughly and left nothing to chance.

Anglers always have spent much more time fishing than they have catching fish, even in bygone days when steelhead were far more numerous and anglers far less so. Such time is never wasted; aside from the sheer pleasure of fishing, even when no fish respond, it affords the opportunity for practice and experiment, for observation and contemplation, and for learning. These quiet, introspective periods, which always have accounted for most of our hours astream, remain one of the chief attractions of fly fishing, largely responsible for its restorative powers.

But today, with fewer fish and more fishermen, these quiet periods tend to be longer and more frequent, and anglers have responded by finding new ways to derive satisfaction and reward from them. In my case this has meant redefining the very way I fish.

This I have done by giving up the longer rods and heavier lines I once used (even these were smaller and lighter than those used by most steelhead anglers) in favor of a very light seven-foot rod and floating line. This combination, now used for most of my summer fishing, requires wading in places I would probably avoid if I were still using a longer rod and heavier line; this, in turn, has added much to the challenge of wading, which I have always enjoyed.

The small rod and light line also force me to exercise more care with every cast and to be much more precise in handling and mending line, and I find this adds much to the pleasure of casting.

Some anglers might consider these things impediments or handicaps, but fly fishing by its very nature requires acceptance of self-imposed handicaps, and for me they simply make the sport more interesting. I can spend many long hours on a summer river using such tackle and methods, catch nothing, and still come away feeling I have had a full and satisfying day.

True, such light tackle would be out of place on rivers larger than those I usually fish, but only by a matter of degree. I think it is always possible to add to the challenge and enjoyment of fishing by using the smallest, lightest tackle allowable under the circumstances. If an angler chooses to do this, I also think it will make him a better fisherman.

Of course there are still days when I catch a fish, or sometimes two, and rare occasions when I catch more. On one memorable day, not very many seasons ago, fourteen steelhead came to my fly and I managed to land and release nine of them—and believe me, fighting fourteen steelhead in a single day really tires you out. The next day I went out and released five more. Last season's best was a four-fish day, but that wasn't bad; there have been other seasons when a single fish was the best I could do on any day.

The occasional multiple-fish day proves only that in steelhead fly fishing, as in almost everything else, it helps to be in the right place at the right time. It's also probably a good thing such days come only rarely; with all the other pleasures fishing gives, they amount to an embarrassment of riches, more than any angler should want.

But they also amount to something more: a reward for persistence and an affirmation that in lean times my reason for being on the river is still a valid one, that all the hours, all the effort, all the thousands of fishless casts are still worth it—because the very next cast may bring a fish that justifies everything.

That hope is what keeps me going. As long as I know there is still a chance for success—if not every day, or even every week, then eventually—that's enough to fuel my seasonal passion.

THE MAN FROM
CAMPBELL RIVER

A LIBRARY, it would seem, is about as far from a trout stream as it's possible to get. Trout streams are always lively and busy and noisy; libraries, by their very nature, are eternally quiet, and within their precincts everything seems to move at a glacial pace. The air always feels clean on a trout stream, clear and redolent with the scents of the surrounding forest; a library smells mostly of old books.

Yet libraries also offer many opportunities for anglers, for they are the repositories of the fishing in print—the recorded culture, history, tradition, and technology of the sport, the fount of all fly-fishing knowledge. Most libraries also have "special collections," a place where they house their most rare and precious books, manuscripts, and historic records, and these sometimes provide even greater treasures for inquisitive anglers.

The rooms containing a library's special collections typically lie behind a thick door with an electronic lock that can be opened only from the inside, unless you have the combination. To gain entry you may have to surrender your driver's license and sign a form authorizing the temporary waiver of at least several of your civil rights. It's

66

probably a little like trying to gain admission to the Pentagon command center. The fuss is worth it, though, because special collections are like gold mines for writers or researchers. Even when the subject is fly fishing.

The fine special collections at the library of the University of British Columbia in Vancouver are an example. Here, among other treasures, you will find the original manuscripts, notes, and correspondence of Roderick Haig-Brown, in my opinion the greatest fishing writer of his generation, perhaps of any generation. His twenty-seven books—most written in the spacious study of his riverside home in Campbell River, British Columbia—were for me a continuing source of inspiration, and his lyrical prose style became the model for my own literary voice when I began writing. Most of his nonfiction works were about fly fishing and conservation, but he also wrote novels, for both adults and young people, and essays on a wide range of subjects—the passing of the age of steam, thoughts on law, education, and war, observations on animals and wildlife, even libraries and librarians.

Haig-Brown's fishing books, including *The Western Angler*, *A River Never Sleeps*, the famous "four seasons" books—*Fisherman's Winter*, *Fisherman's Spring*, *Fisherman's Summer*, and *Fisherman's Fall*—were notable for some of the most vivid, lyrical prose ever to grace the printed page, and it was mostly those books that earned their author a deserved place in the annals of English literature.

But Haig-Brown was more than a writer; he was also a leader. He served as a magistrate, army officer, and chancellor of the University of Victoria. He also was an activist, alerting the people of British Columbia to the need to conserve their natural resources. By any measure, that's an impressive résumé, and it's tempting to say that Haig-Brown was the very model of a modern renaissance man. Such a role may have come naturally to him, considering his family and educational background in England, but it also reveals a man of powerful intellect, which is an absolute prerequisite for becoming a successful writer.

He also was an extraordinarily sensitive man, one who felt things strongly and sensed how others felt, and thus he was able to write with great feeling. He was blessed with great natural curiosity and interest in the world around him and spent a great deal of time observing it and thinking about what he saw. These are also necessary qualifications for a writer, especially one whose chief topic was nature—for such was Haig-Brown's chief topic, although he usually approached it from the perspective of a fisherman. That he did so was only natural, because it's axiomatic that writers should write about the things they know best, and Haig-Brown was already an experienced fly fisher when he came to this country from his native England; thus he saw it through the eyes of a fisherman, and it was from that vantage point that he mainly wrote.

He also loved books, and a writer must love books. You can't expect to write well until you've read the works of others who have written well, and Haig-Brown was devoted to books all his life. In fact, it was this devotion that first brought him in contact with Ann Elmore, the woman who would become his wife. She was working in a Seattle bookstore when they met, and their mutual interest in books was one of the things that bound them together through all their years of marriage. Anyone who has visited the book-filled study of Haig-Brown House in Campbell River can testify to the breadth and depth of their literary interests.

So by the time he embarked on his literary career, Haig-Brown already possessed many of the requirements of a successful writer—great natural talent, a keen intellect, sensitivity, strong powers of observation, a developing knowledge of a particular subject—nature or the outdoors, in his case—and a broad exposure to the works of other writers. But even with all this going for him, he still had to serve a literary apprenticeship, spending the time necessary to develop his craft and define his own literary style.

He started in England with *Silver*, a children's book about the life history of the Atlantic salmon. Next came a novel, *Pool and Rapid*, based on his early years on Vancouver Island, and then, in 1939, *The Western Angler*, his first true fishing book. It also was the book that brought Haig-Brown to attention in North America, but that had less to do with literary excellence than with the fact it was really the first book to describe the abundant angling opportunities of the Pacific Northwest. The original manuscript in the University of British Columbia special collections clearly shows that when he wrote it, Haig-Brown was still searching for his literary voice.

Paging through that manuscript and Haig-Brown's other records was for me an almost eerie experience. It made me feel slightly guilty, as if I were prowling through his desk drawers while he was out of the room, or as if I were poking around in the rafters of his brain, eavesdropping on the creative process. Either seemed an egregious violation of his privacy—and yet I assume that by giving his papers to the library, he or his family intended for them to be made available for inquiring minds like mine.

Haig-Brown never learned to master the typewriter. All his books were written in longhand with a fountain pen, filling scores of ruled notebooks, the same type of composition book once popular with elementary-school students. Most or all his final manuscripts were typed by his wife, Ann. The original handwritten manuscript of *The Western Angler* shows many corrections—sentences lined out, words or phrases inserted, marginal notes, and so on—not frenzied, agonizing edits like those found on the score of a Beethoven symphony, but calm, deliberate attempts to craft a better phrase or evoke a clearer image.

One notebook indicates Haig-Brown considered several alternative titles for *The Western Angler*. Among them: *Western Trout and Pacific Salmon*; *The Rise at Sunset*; *Salt, Swift, and Still*; *Green Waters*; *The Evening Rise*; or "some such title as '*Angling Economics*' or '*Sustained Yield*' or '*Fish for All*'." He added: "Don't care for any of these, but a good one might be the soundest bet from the point of view of persuading the bookseller." How he arrived at the final title is not explained in his notes. Perhaps it was supplied by the publisher, the late and greatly lamented Derrydale Press, which published *The Western Angler* in a beautiful, deluxe two-volume edition of 950 copies.

Two years later, in 1941, Haig-Brown published *Return to the River*, and it was immediately obvious the young author had finally found his literary voice. *Return to the River* is, of course, a novel, and it would be less than candid to say it is distinguished for its structure, plot, dialogue, or characterizations; it is not. What makes it extraordinary, what sets it apart from anything Haig-Brown had written previously, is its abundance of lush, lyrical prose. Here, for the first time, the full power of Haig-Brown's descriptive writing was visible, the kind of writing that was to establish him as a literary figure of the very first rank.

Consider, for example, this passage:

"The water was a little colored, not muddy but less clear than during the brilliance of its summer flow, and brought with it fallen leaves and twigs and dead fir needles. Most of the leaves twisted and swam and swirled a few inches below the surface—alder leaves, some black and rightly fallen, others still green, torn from the trees by winds that had brought the fall rains; maple leaves, sodden, dark brown and fast breaking up; willow leaves, long and slender, some yellow, some black. Under the leaves, deeper in the water, were the salmon."

I defy anyone to read those words without forming a vivid image of the scene, or without being caught up in its poetic rhythm.

Here's another example, one of my favorites:

"The warm wind passed upstream, sighing with its freight of rain, finding always a stronger gust of itself to shatter the big drops from leaves that still held them. It swayed the tall firs almost gently, loading them with water, trembling the water from them again minutes later. Drenched with water, the dark leaves of salal and rhododendron shone and quivered and dripped in penetrated shelter down under the tall trees. The clouds rolled up, white and gray and soft, climbing the valley and misting into the mountains . . . The creeks talked on the hillsides, turning brown and foamy and tumbling faster in their rocky beds."

We who live in the Pacific Northwest are surely among the world's foremost experts on wind and rain, but I think even the most wind-blown and rain-soaked among us would agree that no one has ever penned a better description of our usual weather.

In 1946, Haig-Brown published *A River Never Sleeps*, now judged the finest of all his fishing books. The handwritten manuscript of that book, also in the University of British Columbia collection, shows surprisingly few corrections, and it seems amazing that such beautiful prose could flow from the mind through the hand to the paper with so little need for revision. If anything, his words evoked even more vivid images than those contained in *Return to the River*. Consider his description of steelhead fishing:

"The steelhead, with the brightness of the sea still on him, is livest of all the river's life. When you have made your cast for him, you are no longer a careless observer. As you mend the cast and work your fly well down to him through the cold water, your whole mind is with it, picturing its drift, guiding its swing, holding it where you know he will be. And when the shock of his take jars through you to your forearms and you lift the rod to its bend, you know that in a moment the strength of his leaping body will shatter the water to brilliance, however dark the day."

Or this account of a mountain sunset:

"The mountains were clear in the sunlight; they are clear still, yet somehow veiled by the lesser light of the sinking sun. Soon the snow slides will be colored with sunset, not pink, though pink is the word that means some part of the color, but flushed and glowing with the reflection of clean, bright flame."

But again he had to search for the right title. A notebook with out-lines, notes, and ideas for the book is labeled *A Year of Fishing Days*, apparently the name Haig-Brown used to refer to the work while it was in progress.

The handwritten manuscript of *A River Never Sleeps* fills several notebooks. The original typescript also is in the UBC special collections, so it's easy to follow the creative process all the way through and see how Haig-Brown developed his ideas from written notes and refined his prose until it had just the mood or inflection he desired. A good example is the evolution of the famous last paragraph of the book, perhaps the most oft-quoted passage in all Haig-Brown's writings. This is how it appears in the original handwritten manuscript, including his corrections:

"I still don't know why I fish or why other men fish, except that we like it and it makes us think and feel. But I do know that if it were not for the strong, quick life of rivers, for their sparkle in the sunshine, for the cold greyness of them under rain, and the feel of them about my legs as I set my feet hard down on rocks or sand or gravel, I should fish less often. A river is never quite silent; it can never, of its very nature, be quite still; it is never quite the same from one day to the next. It has its own life and its own beauty and the creatures [here he originally wrote 'that depend on it,' then crossed it out] it nourishes are live and beautiful [here he later inserted the word 'also']. Perhaps fishing is, for me, only an excuse to be near rivers; if so, I'm glad I thought of it."

The paragraph is followed by a broad, bold dash across the page, perhaps an exclamation of relief or satisfaction at having finished the manuscript.

The typescript version of the same paragraph includes a couple of other changes; whether they were made by Haig-Brown or by an anonymous copy editor preparing the typescript for publication is not clear. But the spelling of "greyness" was changed to "grayness," and the last sentence was broken into two sentences, becoming: "Perhaps fishing is, for me, only an excuse to be near rivers. If that is so, I'm glad I thought of it."

Somewhere along the line, another change was made, for when the book was published the final sentence read: "If so, I'm glad I thought of it." And thank goodness; removing the awkward and unnecessary words "that is" made the sentence a thousand times more effective.

These may seem like small changes, but that's how the writing process works—many small changes, little edits here and there, shaping, polishing, refining the manuscript until it has just the right feel or inflection. It's not much different from making adjustments to a new fly pattern until it proves itself effective.

All of Haig-Brown's subsequent fishing books featured the same sort of lyrical prose, but it wasn't confined merely to his books about fishing. For example, when he wrote *The Living Land*, a remarkable inventory of the natural resources of British Columbia, he offered this definition of the meaning of conservation:

"Conservation is a dynamic, not a static, conception. It does not mean simply hanging onto things, like a miser to his gold. It means putting them to use, seeking a valuable return from them and at the same time ensuring future yields of at least equal value. It means having enough faith in the future to respect the future and the needs of future people; it means accepting moral and practical restraints that limit immediate self-interest; it means finding a measure of wisdom and understanding of natural things that few peoples have attained; ultimately, though we no longer see it in this way, it is a religious concept—the most universal and fundamental of all such concepts, the worship of fertility to which man has dedicated himself in every civilization since his race began."

Instructional books about fly fishing are generally the dreariest form of angling literature, but Haig-Brown's *A Primer of Fly Fishing* stands alone because of his application of the same seamless literary style. Fly fishing, he said, "is undoubtedly the best and finest of all forms of fishing, making the strongest demands on the attention and understanding of its followers and yielding in return the greatest and richest rewards; but in this it is exactly the same as the best in music, painting, literature or anything else. Men from every conceivable walk of life are fly fishermen, and good ones, for nothing but individual choice limits membership in the brotherhood."

I might point out that those words were written in the early 1960s, and I think it's likely that if he were writing today, Haig-Brown would be careful to include women among the ranks of fly fishers.

But enough examples. What is it about these words that make them so meaningful and emotionally charged? What technique did Haig-Brown use to make his work so appealing? Or, to put it another way, how did he set the hook and play us as readers?

Well, to begin with, Haig-Brown's prose is always uncomplicated. He said things in the simplest way possible, so there could never be any doubt about his meaning. This seems an obvious thing for any writer to do, yet it can often be devilishly difficult; even the most experienced writer struggles to make things easy for the reader, and many writers fall short of that goal. To be able to write in a simple, uncomplicated fashion may, in fact, be more a function of natural talent than any amount of learning or experience, for it has often been said that the true measure of a genius is in the simplicity of his or her expression.

Repetition is another technique Haig-Brown used when he wanted to drive home a point. His definition of conservation in *The Living Land* serves as a good example, especially when he said that conservation "means having enough faith in the future to respect the future and the needs of future people." The word "future" appears three times in that single short phrase, and you can't read it and go away without thinking about the future, which of course is exactly what he wanted you to be thinking about.

Haig-Brown also loved alliteration, or the use of similar sounds in a sequence. Consider, for example, the repeated F- and B-sounds when he wrote that the creeks were "turning brown and foamy and tumbling faster in their rocky beds," or the repeated L-sounds when he said "The steelhead . . . is livest of all the river's life," or the sequence of S's when he said "the mountains were clear in the sunlight; they are clear still, yet somehow veiled by the lesser light of the sinking sun." He used these sounds almost as if they were musical notes, and indeed alliteration is a technique often used by composers of music, and it works just as well in writing. If it sounds right, it reads right, and Haig-Brown's frequent and successful use of alliteration surely added to the impact of his words.

There are other similarities between musical composition and writing, and one of the most obvious is the use of rhythm or cadence. I don't know if Haig-Brown was a student of music, but he often wrote with a very deliberate rhythm, and I suspect he did so purposely. Repeated use of the word "future" in his definition of conservation is one example; in fact, the whole paragraph containing that definition has a steady and distinctive cadence. The same sort of rhythm is apparent in nearly all of Haig-Brown's later works; you may not always be aware of it, but it's always there, reaching out to satisfy some inner need that we all have, perhaps subconsciously driven by the beating of our own hearts.

Another distinctive feature in Haig-Brown's writing is his use of what I call "action" words. By that I mean there was nothing wimpy in his choice of descriptive terms. He used adjectives like "bold," "strong," "live," and "brilliant," often linking them in alliterative fashion.

What's so special about that? Perhaps the best way to gauge its impact is to look for a moment at the work of another writer. Some years ago an absolutely fascinating book called *Reeling in Russia* was published by Fen Montaigne, a former correspondent for the *Philadelphia Inquirer.* The book is an account of Montaigne's months-long fishing journey all the way across Russia from the Baltic to the Pacific, and while Montaigne isn't much of a fisherman, the chronicle of his adventures will keep any reader turning the pages. His book makes wonderful reading until he begins trying to describe the wilds of Siberia, one of the greatest wilderness areas left on the planet, and here his powers of description utterly fails him. He tells of forests that are dark, waters that are blue, and mountains that are snow-capped—all bland, watery clichés that convey nothing of the majesty of that great land.

Imagine how Haig-Brown would have described those scenes. I suspect his Siberian mountains would have been brushed with that same "clean, bright" sunset flame, or maybe something even more vivid. I'm certain he would have found the Siberian rivers bright, brilliant, and full of quick life, and his Siberian forests would have stood out boldly against the endless sky. I think the point is clear.

So those are some of the techniques Haig-Brown used to construct the word-pictures that first appealed to his readers seventy-five years ago and still appeal to us today. But he could never have constructed such images out of whole cloth; he had to have the experiences to back them up. So when he wrote of that mountain sunset, he was surely thinking of a sunset he had seen, and when he described steelhead with the brightness of the sea still on them, he was undoubtedly thinking of fish he had actually held in his hands. He used the techniques of a writer to recreate these scenes and offer clues that would help readers construct their own versions. When a reader does this, he or she also naturally relies on experience, so when Haig-Brown says "clean, bright flame," the reader is likely to remember a sunset just like that and say, yes, that's exactly the way it was. It doesn't matter that the image Haig-Brown had in mind might be very different from the one the reader has summoned from memory; both are just as vivid and just as personal in the eye of the beholder.

And that, I think, is the real secret of Haig-Brown's prose: He described things in ways that bring our own memories to life, and that's why his writing seems so alive, so compelling, and so emotionally powerful. He awakens the best of our own recollections, stirs the depths of our imaginations, and brings light to our mind's eye.

I don't know whether Haig-Brown did this intentionally or merely by instinct, although I suspect it was a little of both. But it doesn't really matter; the fact is that he did it, and everyone who reads his work is better for it.

"Perhaps fishing is, for me, only an excuse to be near rivers," he said. "If so, I'm glad I thought of it." I suspect for Roderick Haig-Brown, fishing was a great deal more than only an excuse to be near rivers. I think it also was a way for him to write about the natural world, as only a fly fisherman could see it.

If so, we can all be glad he thought of it.

CALM, COOL, AND COLLECTED

A LONG time ago I decided never to become a collector of fly-fishing books. I made that decision after witnessing what happened to several friends who became collectors. They started spending less time fishing and a lot more time in pursuit of books, especially rare old ones, until at last they stopped fishing altogether. Their addiction to books had become so absorbing, so obsessive, so all-consuming, and so expensive that they had no time or money left for fishing. Worse yet, they didn't even seem to miss it.

That was a fate I desperately wanted to avoid.

But I soon discovered it wasn't easy to resist becoming a collector. My wife, Joan, worked in the book department of a major department store, so there were nearly always new fly-fishing books under the Christmas tree or at birthdays. Other people gave me books, and I bought quite a few myself. Later, when I began writing fly-fishing book reviews for several publications, I started receiving many new books directly from publishers. After the reviews were written, I donated nearly all those books to charities, but a few inevitably found their way into my fishing library, which continued growing despite my best intentions.

After decades in Seattle, we moved to Whidbey Island in northern Puget Sound. I was still unpacking things when my friend Dale Broughton visited, inspected the space designated for an office in our new home, and volunteered to build bookshelves along one wall, just because he enjoys doing things like that. I gratefully accepted his offer, which resulted in a series of handsome pine shelves with more than sixty linear feet of space.

The many boxes of fishing and history books (history being another great love of mine) I had brought from Seattle easily filled all that space, with no room to spare. That meant I would soon face the dilemma of what to do if I wanted to add a new book to my library. The only way to make room for it would be to remove a book already on the shelf, and I knew the time would soon come when that challenge would have to be faced.

Which it did. So I began a merciless sort of triage, culling older volumes and replacing them with new ones I thought of greater value or importance. These choices were always difficult, but each time I was forced to make one I also silently congratulated myself for successfully resisting the urge to become a book collector. As long as I had limited shelf space, my library would never be able to grow any larger than it already was, and I still had the time, energy, money—and, most important, the desire—to go fishing.

Until then, I'd never gotten around to counting the number of fly-fishing books in my library, though my estimate was somewhere around 200. So when I finally did take an inventory, it was a great shock to discover the actual number was 425. No matter how you slice it, a library that size has to qualify as a collection, and those handsome pine shelves were beginning to bow under the weight of those 425 volumes.

I'm still not sure how this happened, but it was clear I had become a book collector despite my best intentions. That it occurred slowly, almost painlessly, and without my even realizing it was, I suppose, a good thing. I hadn't fallen victim to the collecting urge as much as some of my friends, who gave up not only fishing but also much of their income to pursue books. If one is fated to become a book collector, I suppose I had unwittingly discovered the easiest way to go about it.

The discovery that I had so many books also made me curious as to exactly what was in my collection, so I decided to take a closer look at its contents. I found many works on fisheries biology and genetics, several weighty tomes on aquatic entomology, and several others on stream management—all essential references for someone who wants to write about fishing. I also found numerous books about fly-tying techniques and fly patterns, a good selection of works on fly-fishing history and literature, and many volumes describing fly-fishing tactics for various species of fish in various types of water.

The authors most often represented among the large selection of books about fly tying and fly patterns included Kenneth E. Bay, George F. Grant, Eric Leiser, Art Lingren, and Richard Talleur. Works by John McDonald, Paul Schullery, John Waller Hills, Alfred Joshua Butler, and William Radcliffe topped my collection of books about fly-fishing history. There were many books on saltwater fly fishing by a great many authors, but the inimitable Lefty Kreh topped the list with five titles. Six volumes by the late Charles E. Brooks made him the most prolific of a large number of authors of books about stream fishing and tactics. Trey Combs ranked first for steelhead, with three books, and if there is such a thing as all-around fly-fishing miscellany, then Dave Hughes was my champion with five titles, each exploring a different aspect of the sport.

But the largest number of books were those I vaguely defined as "just good reading"—the kind of books best perused in front of the fireplace on a winter evening, perhaps with a snifter of brandy for accompaniment. They were books describing the experiences, contemplations, introspections, and philosophies of other anglers, books calculated to inspire and entertain.

Among these authors, Roderick Haig-Brown was by far the most often represented, with seventeen titles. That was no surprise; Haig-Brown is my all-time favorite angling writer and literary inspiration. My old friend (and several times publisher) Nick Lyons was next, with eight titles. Other writers in the same "just good reading" category included John Gierach (even though I once referred to him in a review as master of the "smart-ass" school of fly-fishing writing), Russell Chatham, Arnold Gingrich, William Humphrey, Dana Lamb, Ben Hur Lampman, Robert Traver, and W. D. Wetherell, each represented by at least three titles. There were quite a few other authors who contributed one or two books.

Most of these are American writers, but my library also includes many works from the United Kingdom, Canada, New Zealand, Australia, and France. New Zealand in particular has produced some fine fly-fishing authors—O. S. "Budge" Hintz, John Parsons, and Tony Jenson, to mention just a few.

Most of the books in my library date from the late twentieth or early twenty-first century, though a few date back to the nineteenth century.

Many of my books were autographed by their authors. Most collectors treasure works signed by their authors because it makes them more valuable on the commercial market, a matter of great importance to collectors who consider books as investments. That's especially true if the author who signed the book is no longer living. I couldn't care less about the commercial value of the books in my collection—I have always considered them an investment in knowledge and enjoyment, not a financial investment—and nearly all my autographed books were gifts. With only one or two exceptions, I have never asked another author to sign a book.

One reason I haven't is that I think signing books is one of the most difficult things a writer is ever asked to do. I don't mean just signing one's name; that's easy (unless you have to sign it 2,000 times, as a publisher once asked of me). The difficulty comes when someone asks for more than just a signature, such as a personal inscription for him- or herself, or for Dear Old Uncle Harry or somebody. It's always a challenge to think of something fresh, original, or personal to say under such circumstances, and I can't imagine anything that can cause a faster attack of writer's block. I don't believe I'm alone in this, either, because—let's face it—most authors' personal inscriptions are hopelessly inane, and I suspect it's because they couldn't quickly think of anything else to say.

I know. I'm as guilty of this as any other writer. To avoid inanity—or to avoid the awkward pause that always follows a request for a personal inscription while I'm trying desperately to think of something worthwhile to say—I've developed a certain number of stock phrases and inscriptions I've used many times in many books. But I don't like doing that, either, because I'm always worried that some readers will end up comparing books and discover that what they thought was an original inscription written just for them is exactly the same as the inscription in someone else's book.

I think the late Arnold Gingrich had a good solution to this problem. My copy of his book, *The Joys of Trout*, contains this inscription: *For Steve Raymond, Fraternally, Arnold Gingrich.* That was it—short, succinct, easy, and right to the point. But Arnold's solution unfortunately doesn't work in every case, because when someone who's just bought one of your books asks you to "write something about sea-run cutthroat fishing" in it, he's probably not going to settle just for "fraternally." And if the person who wants you to sign the book is a woman—well, "fraternally" just isn't going to work.

It's especially difficult to think of something appropriate to say for someone you've never met, but it does help if you've at least heard something about him or her. I was once asked to sign a book for Tiger Woods, and although I'd never met him, I knew who he was. So I wrote an inscription thanking him for encouraging people to play golf because it keeps them off the streams.

I remember another time an angler showed me a book he had purchased only because he thought I had signed it. Something about the inscription made him suspicious, however, and he asked me to confirm the autograph was genuine. It took only a glance inside the book to determine that someone had forged my signature, and very badly at that. Adding insult to injury, he had then written "Good fishing!" Please! Even I would never stoop to such crass inanity. I placed my genuine signature under the forgery, parenthetically added "the real one," and returned the book to its owner.

A book I once owned offered proof that authors' inscriptions sometimes unwittingly turn out to be even more personal than intended. The store where my wife worked once hosted a book signing by Richard Nixon before he was elected president, and she thought I might like to have a signed copy of his book *Six Crises*. Nixon obligingly signed his name, but also inadvertently left a piece of his breakfast pastry stuck to the signature page. I don't know if that would have made the book more valuable to a collector, and I never tried to find out; I gave the book away long ago.

Many of the autographed books in my library contain typically inane inscriptions, but there are also some pretty good ones, and a few that have special meaning for me. The late Stanley Bascom, who, under the pseudonym Milford Poltroon, edited the extremely funny "piscatorial periodical" known as *The Wretched Mess News*, sent me a copy of his 1971 book, *How to Fish Good*, with the following inscription: "Steve! This is the best book I ever wrote. Milf Poltroon." At the time it also was the *only* book he'd ever written. Milf and I had some good times together and I wrote a number of goofy stories for the *Wretched Mess*. Since I lived in Washington State, he always identified me as his "Washington correspondent."

E. H. "Polly" Rosborough, the famous, talented, and sometimes irascible Oregon fly tyer, published several editions of his book, *Tying and Fishing the Fuzzy Nymphs*. I don't now remember what I said, but evidently I reviewed one of the early editions in less than glowing terms, so when Polly published the fourth edition he sent me a copy inscribed: "May this time meet with your approval."

As I recollect, it did.

Ralph Wahl's *One Man's Steelhead Shangri-La* is his memoir of a great stretch of steelhead water on the Skagit River, now long gone, and a copy of the published work occupies a place on one of my shelves. Right next to it is a copy of the original typescript of the book bearing this inscription by Ralph: "Steve: You were born a generation too late. I would have been delighted to share it with you." Of course he *did* share it, vicariously, through his words and vivid descriptions. As one of my steelhead fishing mentors, he also shared much more—the gift of his priceless knowledge.

My copy of Sparse Grey Hackle's classic *Fishless Days, Angling Nights* is not autographed, but it does include a letter from Sparse (whose real name was Alfred W. Miller). The letter, on stationery from the Anglers Club of New York, was written after I reviewed his book in *The Flyfisher* magazine. "Thank you kindly for giving me a generous and friendly review," he said. "It was gracious of you and I appreciate it very much." That was a much nicer letter than the kind I usually got from authors whose books I had reviewed.

I never met Sparse in person, much to my regret, but he occasionally corresponded with my friend Al Severeid, who shared many of his letters with me. Severeid, incidentally, was one of those highly addicted book collectors mentioned earlier, one who eventually quit fishing in favor of books.

My copy of Lefty Kreh's *Fly Fishing in Salt Water* bears a rather standard inscription: "For Steve Raymond—I hope that this book helps you catch many of these grand fish. All the best, Lefty Kreh." But Lefty added something else, something very special—a fly taped to the page, with this notation: "A favorite baby tarpon fly of the author, tied by Lefty for Steve." It's a handsome fly, and I can scarcely think of anything more personal that an author could add to an inscription. If only I were a better fly tyer, and not so ashamed of my ragged-looking patterns, this might be a solution to the problem of what to say when I'm asked for a personal inscription. I could just sign my name and paste a fly in the book.

Unfortunately, that won't work for me.

Maybe, if the publishing industry continues to shift toward electronic books, I won't have to worry about personal inscriptions any more. I'm definitely no fan of electronic books, but as far as I know, nobody has yet figured out a way to sign names or write personal inscriptions on them.

My book collection also contains a number of unusual and elaborate works, mostly gifts from other writers. One is Van Gorman Egan's *Tyee: The Story of the Tyee Club of British Columbia*, the wonderful chronicle of this famous fishing club. Published by the Ptarmigan Press of Campbell River, BC, in a limited edition of 180 copies, the book is slipcased and bound in leather fiber with gold foil imprints and was signed by Van Egan and Ann Kask, the graphic designer.

Another rare and unusual little book in my library is Vernon S. (Pete) Hidy's *An Open Letter to the International Society of Flymph Fishermen*, signed by the author. I didn't even know there was such a society, or that I had been "accepted" into membership, until I received this copy, number thirty-three of a limited edition of one hundred.

Pete Hidy appeared on the fly-fishing scene in 1941 with publication of James Leisenring's *The Art of Tying the Wet Fly, as told to V. S. Hidy*. Leisenring was a Pennsylvania master angler and fly tyer, and Pete's fascination with his theories led to publication of the 1941 work and several reprints. An expanded edition, *The Art of Tying the Wet Fly and Fishing the Flymph*, was published in 1971, with three new chapters about the "flymph" written by Hidy. The "flymph" is a fly pattern designed to simulate the appearance of a hatching nymph surrounded by an air bubble as it makes its way to the surface.

The *Open Letter* includes two "flymphs" tied by Hidy along with samples of the dubbing material used in their construction. It even includes a toothpick for the reader to insert through the eye of one of the flies so he or she can then submerge the fly in a glass of water and see what it looks like. Not many books come complete with dubbing material or a toothpick, and I've seen copies of this one listed for as much as five hundred dollars in dealer's catalogs. You'll never see mine listed there.

Hidy, who passed away in 1983, also favored the angling community with another book, *The Pleasures of Fly Fishing*, published in 1972, and edited the treasured works of Ben Hur Lampman in two wonderful little volumes, *A Leaf from French Eddy* and *Where Would You Go?* He deserves far more attention than he has received among the angling literati.

Some other rare items on my bookshelves:

The Greased Line, edited by John Alevras, Joe Brown, and Alec Jackson, is a collection of excerpts from four decades of the newsletter published by the Washington Steelhead Flyfishers. Richly illustrated with color photographs, it includes pieces written by such steelhead fly-fishing legends as Wes Drain, Syd Glasso, Bill McMahon, Walt Johnson, Al Knudson, and others. My copy is not numbered, but my late friend Alec Jackson, one of the editors, told me only fifty copies were printed.

Totem Topics, edited by Ron Grantham, is not quite as rare or elaborate as *The Greased Line*, but it contains excerpts from a newsletter published by the Totem Flyfishers of British Columbia. My copy is the club's twenty-fifth anniversary edition (1993), a handsome hardbound book dedicated to the memory of Roderick Haig-Brown. It includes segments by such BC fly-fishing luminaries as Jim Kilburn, Pete Broomhall, Jim Stewart, Martin Tolley, Jack Vincent, Bill Yonge, Art Lingren, and Lee Straight. There's plenty of good fishing in these pages, along with black-and-white photos and line drawings.

Another rare little gem that somehow ended up in my library is Sam Lehman's *Fly of the Month* calendar for 1972. The calendar includes Sam's hand-colored fly illustrations for each month, on pages bound together with a leather thong. Besides the traditional twelve months, there's a sort of generic additional month that includes "seven extra days . . . to take care of catching up on your fishing, fly tying and similar very essential duties." Old Sam had a good sense of humor.

One of the more spectacular books on my shelves is Jack Heddon's *Scotcher Notes: Bibliographical, Biographical and Historical Notes to George Scotcher's "Fly Fisher's Legacy," circa 1810, with comments on the Fly-Dressings*. Published in 1975 by the Honey Dun Press of London, the book's front matter states that "One Hundred & Sixty-five Copies of this work have been Printed in this format on Abbey Mills Greenfield Laid Paper. One Hundred & Fifty Numbered Copies Signed by the Author & Artist are for Sale. Fifteen Copies are 'Out of Series.'" My copy is one of the latter, numbered IX.

The book is bound in quarter green morocco grained leather with gilt lettering, and the initials of the binder, A. S. Sismore, appear on the inside rear cover. The book includes six hand-colored fly plates by John Simpson, and a real fly—Scotcher's Black Gnat—mounted opposite the title page. The whole package comes in a box with a silk ribbon book marker. This elaborate work was obviously designed to command a high price from well-heeled collectors. In my case, they missed the target, but I'm very glad to have this beautiful little book in my library.

By any measure, the strangest book in my collection is *Saltwater Fly Fishing Fundamentals, An Introduction to Saltwater Fly Fishing*, by Australian writer Peter Morse. It's autographed: "To Steve: I thought you might enjoy this special 'Northern Hemisphere' edition —it's you guys who do it the wrong way round." What he meant by this, and what makes the book so strange, is that this particular copy was bound with the cover upside down and backwards, so the front cover is on the back of the book and vice versa, and if you open the book from what appears to be the front cover, the text is upside down.

Morse's humorous inscription is in the back of the book, because it appears to be the front. But of course it really isn't.

Got all that?

I assume, or at least hope, that all the books in the press run weren't bound this way. If this is the only one—well, who knows how much it might be worth? It might be like some of those postage stamps that were printed with errors, which have brought prices of hundreds of thousands or even millions of dollars on the auction market. Somehow I doubt anyone would bid that much for this odd book; in any case, it's not for sale.

Assuming my copy of Morse's upside-down work isn't unique, then the rarest book in my library, or perhaps any fishing library, is *Bill Nation, a British Columbia Fly-Fishing Legend*. Only three copies exist. The text is a brief (nine-page) biography of Nation, the pioneer British Columbia fishing guide and fly tyer who created a series of Kamloops trout fly patterns used by several generations of anglers. It was written by my friend, BC angling historian Art Lingren, and a ten-page pamphlet version was distributed to attendees at the British Columbia Federation of Fly Fishers' 2000 Annual General Meeting, which was dedicated to Nation. Lingren and another friend, Bill Jollymore, were both instrumental in resurrecting Nation's reputation and heretofore all-but-forgotten fly patterns, and I also tried to do my part. But I didn't know Art and Bill were planning to publish this special edition of Art's text until I received a copy from them.

A hand-laid card in the front of the book tells its story: "Three copies of this work have been hard bound with a Nation fly mounted in the slipcase. A Nation's Red is mounted in the slipcase of the author's copy, a Nation's Green Sedge is mounted in Bill Jollymore's, and a Nation's Special in Steve Raymond's. The author dressed the Nation's Red for copy No. 1 and Bill Jollymore dressed the Nation's Green Sedge and Nation's Special for copies Nos. 2 and 3. Gwen Kushner, of Campbell River, bound copies Nos. 2 and 3, and made all three special slipcases." She also signed them.

I have no idea of the monetary value of this little book, but since only three copies exist it is probably substantial. For that reason, I keep it under lock and key, along with some of my other potentially valuable books. But the book's chief value to me will always be its reminder of the thoughtfulness and generosity of my friends, plus the story it tells of one of British Columbia's greatest fly fishermen.

The books that crowd those sixty feet of shelves in my office contain many other memories—and much more. They enrich the days when I cannot go fishing and their teachings help me on the days I can. Some of them I've read at least a half-dozen times, and they still seem fresh each time I turn to them.

Will books survive in the electronic age that now seems upon us? I think a more relevant question is whether *we* can survive without books. In any case, I believe traditional books, printed on paper and bound between covers, will be with us indefinitely. I think they will survive because their authors can sign them and say whatever they please (or can think of); because we won't need batteries to read them; because we will always need the tactile feedback they give us; and most of all because of their sense of permanence. Electronic books, by their very nature, have none of these features. They do have one advantage, though: They will never develop the musty smell that old books have, although some people grow to like that aroma.

Yet another reason we will always have traditional books is because they sometimes combine the printer's and binder's arts with the writer's prose to make a book something of real and lasting beauty, a work of art unto itself—something like my copy of *Scotcher Notes*, for example. That's also something electronic books will never be able to duplicate.

Take it from someone who ended up a book collector in spite of himself.

THE FORGOTTEN HATCH

It was a glorious day, the first sunny day after an interminable stretch of gray, wet weather. If you're a Pacific Northwest resident, you get used to those long rainy periods. Then, when the sun finally does come out, it makes you blink.

It also was an unusually warm day for early April and the lake was crowded, as I had known it would be. It has been crowded ever since the state declared it a "selective fishing" water. The selective fishing regulations allow only the use of artificial lures or flies with single barbless hooks, with a daily catch limit of one trout exceeding eighteen inches. It's one thing to establish such regulations on a body of water, however, and quite another for the water actually to produce trout of eighteen inches or larger. Many waters don't. The one I had chosen on this April Saturday did, so it was always crowded, especially on warm, sunny weekends.

I shoved off in my nine-foot aluminum pram and looked for an opening in the picket fence of boats and pontoon craft anchored side by side in a long line ahead. All held fishermen who were hunched over, staring fixedly at strike indicators bobbing in the chop. Each indicator was attached to a long leader dangling a chironomid imitation near the lake bottom, waiting for a fish to grab it and pull the strike indicator under.

I steered carefully around the line of boats and headed for the far side of the lake. Not many people are willing to row that far, and it's a long way to kick in a float tube, so it's usually possible to find a place to fish in relative solitude. Once again that proved to be the case.

Even better, I could see a hatch in progress. Small chironomids were popping to the surface and trout were rising leisurely to suck them in. I tied on a favorite chironomid emerger imitation, designed to float in the surface film, and began casting with a six-foot rod. Some people think such little rods are toys and that people who use them are nuts, but there are actually some very good reasons for using such rods to fish floating lines on lakes: A short rod needs only a short casting stroke and generates high line speed, which can shave as much as a second off the time it takes to get your fly over a rising fish if you're using a long rod. That second can be critical when you're fishing to fast-cruising trout. Using a short rod is also a lot more fun.

The chironomid imitation brought about a dozen trout to the surface. I missed half of them—chalk it up to rust from all those rainy winter days—but hooked and landed all the others. The smallest was about sixteen inches; a couple exceeded the eighteen-inch minimum size limit. I could have kept one if I'd wanted. I didn't.

While I fished, I noticed little dimples here and there on the surface. They weren't caused by trout; they looked almost like big raindrops falling on the water. That's the first thing that occurs to you when you live in the Pacific Northwest.

But they weren't raindrops. It took a while to register, but I finally realized I was seeing water boatmen (*Corixidae*) taking flight or returning to the water with nearly the velocity of bullets. Others were just sticking their ugly little rear ends up for a breath of fresh air to take with them back down below. These fast-moving little bugs carry a bubble of air under their abdomens when they return to the depths, like miniature aquatic astronauts. The air lasts them an amazingly long time before they have to return to the surface for more.

Water boatmen are often active on warm days in the late spring and early fall. To see them flying in early April was surprising, but it was the kind of day that if it happened in June, you'd expect to see them.

You don't hear much about water boatmen. Most stillwater anglers probably aren't even aware of them. Maybe that's because even when water boatmen are active, trout rarely seem to get excited about it. In my fly-fishing experience I could remember only a few occasions when trout were feeding selectively on water boatmen.

One of those times I had tied up a few simple imitations on a size 12 hook, lightly weighted to keep the fly under the surface when it was retrieved rapidly on a floating line. The body was dark gray dubbing with a couple of turns of silver tinsel to imitate the silvery air bubble carried underwater by the insect. A mottled pheasant rump feather over the top completed the pattern, matching the colors of the natural and simulating its long, paddle-like legs. The pattern had worked well the first time I tried it and I still had a few in my fly box. So when the chironomid hatch finally petered out but the water boatmen continued blitzing in and out of the water, I decided to try one of the water boatmen imitations.

Nothing happened for the first few casts. It was fun fishing the water boatman imitation, though, because you have to retrieve it in rapid, erratic strokes to match the high-speed maneuvers of the natural. That was a welcome change from fishing the chironomid, which hardly needed to be moved at all.

Then something grabbed the fly hard and was gone just as quickly, leaving a big swirl on the surface. I took it as a note of encouragement.

A couple of casts later another trout socked the fly midway through a retrieve, stretching the line like a rubber band. The leader held, fortunately, and the trout was quickly into the air, leaping repeatedly, then duking it out in a series of short runs punctuated by bouts of head-shaking. When I finally brought it to hand, the fly was stuck deeply in its lower lip. Even with forceps, I had trouble removing it despite the barbless hook.

It went on that way for the next hour. Fish after fish banged the fast-stripped fly, flew into the air, then streaked away. All were in the sixteen- to eighteen-inch class, thick, fat, lively rainbow that were great fun to handle on the little rod. For some reason, they all fought much harder than the trout I'd hooked earlier on the chironomid pattern. It almost seemed as if they were furious someone would try to fool them with a water boatman imitation.

Eventually, however, the dimples from rising and diving bugs slowly began to disappear. The trout began disappearing along with them. The hatch was over, and so was my day of fishing.

I loaded up my boat, drove home, put away my tackle, got out my fly-tying gear, and started tying water boatman imitations. This might be a hatch you don't hear much about, or run into very often, but I wanted to be sure I was ready the next time I did.

LUNDBOM REVISITED

THE FIRST few years Joan and I fished Lundbom Lake, we were treated rather gently by the weather. The place we liked to camp—the rocky point at the lake's east end—offered no shelter from the west winds that gained momentum as they swept the length of the lake, but only once or twice in our experience had the wind been strong enough to interfere with fishing or force us off the lake.

Then everything changed. Sometimes the wind howled for hours on end, sending three- and four-foot waves crashing against the point's rocky shoreline. When that happened, fishing was impossible, so we spent the time exploring the lake's margins, the nearby woods, and the steep grassy slope beyond the rocky point where we camped. During spring the slope was bright with sunflowers, lupine, Nootka rose, and other wildflowers, including a fragile member of the lily family called Indian rice root or Kamchatka lily. The aspen on the point were sometimes visited by mountain bluebirds, their plumage a brilliant match for the sky overhead. Ospreys circled over the lake and ravens called hoarsely from the woods, graceful Bonaparte's gulls dropped in occasionally, and once we saw a pileated woodpecker. At night our camp was favored with blessed silence, interrupted only by the gentle clatter of aspen leaves in the breeze, the yip and yelp of distant coyotes, or the long, eerie chortling of loons.

Wildlife around the lake was abundant. Deer were frequent guests in our camp, and we saw beavers, porcupines, and a handsome badger that looked like a furry armored vehicle.

Lundbom's traveling sedge hatch was one of the best in British Columbia and the lake also had a good spring mayfly hatch, season-long chironomid emergences, and a full complement of dragonflies, damselflies, water boatmen, and leeches, plus all those scuds. It also hosted the greatest falls of flying ants I've ever seen, sometimes several sizes at once. By any measure, Lundbom had everything a fly fisher could want.

Except, perhaps, a pleasant name.

Actually there was one other important thing it lacked, and that worried me: It wasn't remote. The town of Merritt was only ten miles away. At the time it was a sleepy little place, shrouded in perpetual smoke from a local sawmill's wigwam burner, but it had enough people—and probably enough anglers—to overwhelm a lake the size of Lundbom, and I worried that might happen. True, we'd seen few other anglers at the lake, but most of our visits had been before school was out in the spring or after it resumed in the fall, so we were never there when the most visitors could be expected. Nevertheless, we were beginning to see growing evidence of their presence, mostly trash left in fire pits or scattered along the roads and in the woods. I wrote several letters to provincial fish and wildlife officials suggesting Lundbom was such a rare and precious resource it should be protected by appropriate regulations, such as fly fishing only or catch-and-release. Most of my entreaties fell on deaf ears; a few brought responses that were downright hostile.

One June day I witnessed the finest mayfly hatch I'd seen at Lundbom. During a breezy afternoon, big, dark *Callibaetis* duns appeared on the surface and trout began rising to them. I hooked thirteen fish that day, the most ever at Lundbom. By late afternoon, though, the wind-driven swells were approaching dangerous heights. Several other boats were on the lake and I saw two capsize. One was too far away for me to help, but I rushed to the aid of two people who had been thrown into the water from the other. Fortunately, the water was shallow enough they were able to wade ashore, declining any help. But I still faced my own harrowing trip across open water back to our camp, and had a tough time landing the boat without swamping in the heavy surf.

A month later I returned with Joan, Stephanie, and our not-quite-two-year-old son, Randy. This time we were staying at nearby Corbett Lake Country Inn, which had been chosen as headquarters by ABC-TV's *American Sportsman* series for a show on dry-fly fishing for Kamloops trout. I'd been invited to appear on the show with celebrity bandleader Peter Duchin.

After making the producer promise the name of the lake would not be mentioned on television, I suggested we start filming at Lundbom. After the production crew fussed for hours with camera and sound gear, we finally got on the lake late in the afternoon the first day. Peter and I were in a large aluminum jonboat; right behind us, in an even larger jonboat, were the producer, sound man, and photographer. The latter was perched atop a tall stepladder, and we soon discovered that casting a fly isn't exactly easy when there's someone right behind you on a stepladder.

I'd never been in a situation where I was expected to catch fish on demand, and I felt the pressure. It didn't help that Lundbom, always enigmatic, was in a stingy mood that day. A few sedges were on the water and we saw a few scattered rises, but in the hour or so we fished neither of us hooked anything. I felt badly, "but apparently the film crew is used to this sort of thing," I wrote in my diary.

Next day we returned to Lundbom. Shortly before noon the sedges started coming off and fish started rising. I hooked a large trout and quickly broke it off. Then Peter hooked two and broke off both.

Finally I connected with a handsome trout of about two and a half pounds and landed it, our first fish on camera. After a short break for lunch, we resumed fishing in spite of increasing wind. The rise continued and I missed several fish in the chop, but the wind eventually became so strong we called a halt to the fishing day.

I had expected we'd return to Lundbom the following day, but at breakfast the producer announced the previous day's sound recordings were useless "because the steers were bawling all the time." I'd been concentrating so intently on fishing I didn't realize that many cattle were grazing around the lake. Perhaps they were doing only what I remembered Roger LeCompte saying they did to fertilize the lake, but apparently they made lots of noise in the process and I hadn't noticed it. The producer said we'd have to fish somewhere else, and for the remainder of the week we did.

So much for Lundbom Lake's television debut.

My fishing diary contains records of many more visits to Lundbom over a period of years. Once I triumphantly recorded landing seventeen trout, the most I'd ever taken in one day from this tight-fisted water. My best day ever, however, produced only five trout, but the smallest weighed five pounds and two were seven and a half pounds each. It was the kind of day anglers dream about.

Looking back, though, I could see the tenor of my diary entries gradually changing. When I returned to Lundbom the year after the *American Sportsman* trip, I was dismayed to count twenty-seven vehicles parked around the lake, and nearly as many boats on the water. Virtually all the boats had outboard motors and nearly all their occupants were fishing with gang trolls, long unwieldy strings of metal spoons. Many also trailed stringers of small dead trout. It was the manifestation of what I had feared—that this beautiful, productive water was slowly turning into a crowded, noisy, put-and-take fishery.

There were other signs. The fire pits on the rocky point were filled with residue from the great outdoor sport of building fires hot enough to melt beer cans. The grassy slope, where delicate Indian rice root and other wildflowers still struggled to bloom, had been gouged by squadrons of motorized trail bikes. They had left deep gashes that were eroding rapidly, and each heavy rain sent streams of muddy water into the lake.

School was out for the summer by the time of my next visit, and the difference was immediately obvious. Entire villages of campers, mobile homes, and trailers were scattered around the shoreline, and the lake's surface was streaked with speeding boats. Those not speeding were dragging gang trolls and more strings of dead trout. Mindless trail bikers were tearing new ruts in the hillside at the end of the lake, simultaneously fracturing the silence for miles around. I tried fishing, but it's hard to enjoy good sport under such circumstances.

I saw fewer rising trout than ever on that trip, maybe because of the growing oil slicks left on the surface by outboard motors. I suggested as much to another angler who fished the lake often; he agreed there were fewer rising trout but offered a different explanation: "The fish have learned not to stick their heads up for fear of having them ripped off by speeding outboards."

A year later, when I returned, I saw immediately that something had been added to the skyline: A great slash had been cut through the timber on the south side of the lake to make way for the metal towers and thick cables of new power transmission lines. It probably would have been just as easy to place the lines on the far side of the ridge, where they wouldn't have been so visible, but that's not the way things are done in British Columbia.

Canada Day—Canada's equivalent of Independence Day—is July 1, which of course fits hand in glove with America's July 4 holiday. That means both Canadians and Americans flock to the British Columbia interior for a long weekend. It's probably the worst weekend of the year to go fishing, but working people have to take advantage of whatever time they can get away, so, with trepidation, one year

I headed for Lundbom on the Canada Day-July 4th weekend. "There are dozens of rigs camped in every available spot and the lake is taking a fearful pounding," I wrote that night. "I long for those good days when we often camped alone here for days on end. Those days, apparently, are forever gone."

Next day's entry: "Mosquitoes and people equally thick."

A year later, desperate for fishing, and against my better judgment, I returned to Lundbom on the same weekend. It rained hard all night and the day was cold and overcast with a strong west wind. That's probably why the lake was "not as crowded as I've seen it—just counted twenty-six rigs—but crowded enough." People were throwing garbage into the lake, and more noisy trail bikes were tearing up the slope at the east end. There were no more wildflowers.

After that I stayed away from Lundbom for six years. I suppose it was nostalgia that finally prompted me to return—that, coupled with a desire to see the lake once more before the opening of the new Coquihalla Highway. Merritt had always been accessible only by roundabout routes from the populous lower mainland of British Columbia, and for many years that helped protect the fishing; it simply took too long for people to get there. The Coquihalla Highway would follow a direct route to Merritt, and the long-debated project was finally authorized for completion before the opening of the 1986 Vancouver World's Fair. The new highway would reduce driving time to Merritt by hours, and I knew that once it was open the area's lakes would be flooded with anglers.

So I went there on yet another Canada Day weekend in 1985. The first thing I noted in my diary was that "a new road has been punched in, making Lundbom more accessible than ever, which it didn't need to be." And though I was glad to see and fish the lake again, "I also got a sharp reminder of all the things that have kept me away—mindless trail bikers, speedboats, a 'mobile skin-diving school' (of all things), whose members were busy building a dock (probably illegally), loud stereos, and drunken campers. There are still large trout in the lake, as evidenced by large rises and leaping fish, but they are as taciturn as ever."

Next day I fled to another lake, then later returned to Lundbom. "Most of the wild people have left after their three-day weekend and the world is nearly at peace," I wrote. I fished the morning without seeing a fish and then the familiar west wind came up, great screaming gusts of it, and fishing became impossible. I stuck around hoping the wind might subside in the evening, but it didn't.

That night I was kept awake by a nearby party of drunken campers, and next day I drove home. "Very likely this will be the last time I ever come here," I wrote.

Yet I couldn't stay away. Just to see what had finally happened to the place where I'd experienced so many enjoyable days, I made one more trip. It was after the new highway was open and work also had begun to convert the old two-lane highway near Lundbom into a four-lane freeway. I followed the new freeway and came to an interchange with a designated left-turn lane and a lighted overhead sign pointing to Lundbom Lake. The left turn led to a new fifty-mile-an-hour graveled road that took me to the lake in moments. The dirt road around the north side of the lake was still there, however, so I followed it, passing dozens of pickup trucks, campers, motor homes, trailers, a school bus, and other assorted vehicles until I reached the rocky point where I had camped so many times. I couldn't find a parking space there, even though all the aspen on the point had been cut down by campers for green firewood.

At last I found a cramped space off the road, parked, got out, and looked around. Out on the lake I could see several large cabin cruisers, a pair of party barges, several jet skis, even a few small hydroplanes racing back and forth, with outboards screaming. Rock music blared from stereos and ghetto blasters around the shoreline, almost loud enough to obscure the sounds of barking dogs and the shouts of drunken partiers. The usual noisy trail bikes raced up and down the slope at the east end, now totally devoid of vegetation, raising great clouds of dust where fragile lilies once grew.

I left my truck and started climbing a hill, anxious to get away from the irksome racket and dust. When I reached the top, I turned and looked down at the lake. Sunlight glinted from the steel towers and cables of the power lines along the opposite slope and from the metal rooftops of all the campers, trailers, motor homes, buses, and other vehicles parked below. I started counting them but gave up when I reached one hundred.

I realized then that I was viewing the tribal camp of a society that had lost control of itself, hopelessly addicted to internal-combustion engines, ear-damaging noise, and the pursuit of selfish pleasures, without regard for others or the damage they were doing to the earth and its creatures.

With tears in my eyes, I thought of how poor old Angus William Lundbom must have felt watching the destruction of his beloved grasslands. Now I felt the same about the lake that had been given his name.

Unlike Lundbom, however, nobody forced me to leave. I left willingly on my own, and never went back.

BETTER THAN STRAWBERRIES

THERE'S AN old saying that a little knowledge is a dangerous thing. Assuming the truth of that statement, then its logical extension is that a lot of knowledge can be even more dangerous. It can, for example, get you invited to speak to an audience of people who are all more knowledgeable than you are.

That happened to me a few years ago. By then I'd written several fly-fishing books, edited two fly-fishing magazines, and spoken at what seemed like an endless series of fishing-club meetings, conferences, and conclaves. That résumé apparently was what got me invited to speak at a university graduate seminar on ocean resource management, where everyone in the audience would have more education than I did. It occurred to me that it would probably have been more appropriate for me to be listening to them instead of the other way around. However, it did seem probable they hadn't had as much fishing experience as I did, especially with a fly rod, which might give me at least a chance to hold my own. In fact, some of the students— maybe even all of them—might never have been fishing at all.

The seminar was at the University of Washington, my alma mater, and I'd been asked to share my views of how sport fishing should fit into the management of ocean resources. It seemed like a big responsibility, since these future resource managers might never have another opportunity to learn about the cultural and economic importance of sport fishing, or how it should fit into the many demands the world makes on its oceans. For that reason, I spent considerable time researching and preparing what I would say. My research yielded some useful numbers, now long obsolete (they were generated mostly in 1991 and 1996), but I've left them unchanged here because they served so well to illustrate the points I was trying to make and lined up in such a nicely coincidental manner that I was able to use them for a couple of tongue-in-cheek observations.

Somewhat to my surprise, the highly educated young people in the audience seemed very attentive and interested in what I had to say and asked some very good questions. I think we learned from each other, and it was a good experience for me and, I hope, for them.

Here's what I said:

Today is your lucky day. That's because, while the rest of the world is busy getting ready to start another week of work, you get to go fishing. And by fishing I mean, of course, recreational fishing, the kind you do only for fun.

I suppose it's logical to ask whether this is a legitimate topic for a graduate-level course at the University of Washington, or any other university for that matter. After all, in today's world, with an expanding population increasingly dependent on the oceans for food, minerals, oil, commerce, and any number of other essentials, how can one justify "fun" as a legitimate use of the seas? Is it possible to make a case for recreational fishing in the face of all these other seemingly vital competing demands?

I believe there are some good answers to those questions, but before I get to them I think I should first define exactly what I mean when I talk about recreational fishing. We don't know who was first to think of fishing as a form of recreation rather than a means of survival, but we do know it happened a very long time ago. Perhaps it was the Cro-Magnons who left us the stylized drawing of an Atlantic salmon on the wall of a Spanish cave, or maybe it happened even before their time. But whoever first had the idea, it probably came in the form of a sudden realization that once you had caught enough fish for supper, it was still fun to go on catching them—particularly if you used some method other than a spear or a net or a trap, some method that gave the fish more of a fighting chance.

For that is the central idea behind all forms of angling: It requires the acceptance of self-imposed handicaps. If obtaining fish were the only purpose of the exercise, then it would be easier and far more efficient to use dynamite or nets or rotenone or any number of other infernal devices. Instead, anglers use a long rod and a slender line, with bait or lures or artificial flies to entice the fish. This levels the playing field, so to speak, and gives the fish something approaching an equal chance.

It also changes the whole point of the thing: What once was a means to an end becomes instead an end in itself. In other words, it's the fishing that's important, not the catching, and if we succeed in catching fish, that is merely a reward for having fished well. The accomplishment is not the capture of the fish itself, but the skill it took to catch it. And that is the essence of true sport fishing.

In that respect it is rather like golf. If the objective of golf were simply to get the ball in the cup, the easiest way would be to carry it over and drop it in. Instead, golfers handicap themselves by using irons and woods to hit the ball, and by counting the number of strokes it takes them to get the ball into the cup, they measure their skill. So it is with angling.

There are still lots of people who don't understand this, who think the only reason to go fishing is to catch fish. Usually they are people who haven't been at it very long. In fishing, as in nearly everything else, there are several distinct stages of development, and as people pass through those stages and reach maturity, their

motives change and so does their understanding of the whole purpose of the thing.

As fishing has evolved over the centuries, anglers have thought of
more and more sophisticated ways to handicap themselves, until now
I think there is nearly universal agreement that the ultimate form of
sophistication has been reached, and that is fly fishing. Fly fishing
demands physical, intellectual, and observational skills of the highest
order, and together these raise it beyond the realm of sport to something that might even be considered art. I mention this only because
I am a fly fisherman myself—I think it was genetic in my case, since
my father and mother both fished with flies—but, in any case, my
remarks undoubtedly reflect my prejudice.

I can testify that fly fishing is an all-absorbing activity capable of
inspiring mystical, almost religious devotion. Yet in that respect it is
not much different from other forms of angling, even the most primitive; each inspires deep devotion among its followers. The truth of
this is evident in the fact that fishing, especially fly fishing, has produced a more extensive body of literature than any other sport, unless
you consider chess a sport.

As that literature has evolved, many different writers have tried
to answer the question of just what it is about recreational fishing
that makes such fanatics of its followers. I'd like to read some of
their answers, not only because I think they are instructive—and
sometimes amusing—but also because I think they bear directly on
the question of whether recreational fishing is a legitimate use of
the seas.

The first known English text on the subject of fly fishing is usually
attributed to a woman, Dame Juliana Berners, a shadowy figure who
may or may not have lived in England early in the fifteenth century.
Scholars still debate whether she actually wrote the treatise attributed
to her, or whether she actually existed at all, and the truth probably
never will be known for certain, but there is undeniable charm in the

notion that in a sport so long dominated by males, the first one to write about it was a woman.

In any event, Dame Juliana—or whoever wrote the treatise—advised that fishing, and particularly fly fishing, was an "artful" sport, one not to be used "merely for the increasing or saving of your money, but mainly for your enjoyment and to procure the health of your body and, more especially, of your soul." This idea that fishing was good for both your physical and spiritual health has since become one of the most enduring themes of angling literature.

Izaak Walton, who came two centuries after Dame Juliana, was the most famous angling writer who ever lived, and his *Compleat Angler*, first published in 1653, has gone through more editions than any other English-language book except the Bible. We know today that Walton was a plagiarist of the first order, but unlike most plagiarists he considerably improved the material he borrowed from other writers, principally from William Samuel. In Walton's words, the sport of angling was "an employment of one's idle time, which was then not idly spent." And he added this homily, which has since become one of the most famous statements on the nature of sport fishing:

"We may say of angling as Dr. Boteler said of strawberries: 'Doubtless God could have made a better berry, but doubtless God never did;' and so, if I might be judge, God never did make a more calm, quiet, innocent recreation than angling."

Jumping ahead from Walton to the twentieth century, we find some other statements about the appeal of angling. The late Arnold Gingrich, founder of *Esquire* magazine, said that fly fishing "is the most fun you can have standing up." A more eloquent testimony came from the late John Voelker, a Michigan State Supreme Court justice who wrote under the pseudonym Robert Traver and is best known for his novel, *Anatomy of a Murder.* In a piece called "Testament of a Fisherman," Voelker wrote:

"I fish because I love to; because I love the environs where trout are found, which are invariably beautiful, and hate the environs where crowds of people are found, which are invariably ugly; because of all the television commercials, cocktail parties, and assorted social posturing I thus escape; because, in a world where most men seem to spend their lives doing things they hate, my fishing is at once an endless source of delight and an act of small rebellion; because trout do not lie or cheat and cannot be bought or bribed or impressed by power, but respond only to quietude and humility and endless patience . . . because bourbon out of an old tin cup always tastes better out there; because maybe one day I will catch a mermaid; and, finally, not because I regard fishing as being so terribly important but because I suspect that so many of the other concerns of men are equally unimportant—and not nearly so much fun."

Another writer, whose name escapes me now, has said that on the cosmic scale of things, fishing—especially fly fishing—should not be considered any more important than life, death, sex, or drugs.

So what we have here is a mixed bag of ideas and observations: that recreational fishing is good for your physical and spiritual health, that it is a calm, restorative activity, that it has deep connections with nature, that it gets us closer to what's real and farther away from what's not, that it's as good as strawberries and as important as life or death. And those are all reasons why people are devoted to fishing.

What does this have to do with the question of whether sport fishing is a legitimate use of ocean resources? I think the common denominator in all these different observations is that angling is a quality-of-life issue. It's another way of saying that you can mine the oceans for all the food, minerals, and energy you might want, but if that's *all* you have, then you're merely surviving, not living. In order to live, you need to get in touch with nature, and from the point of view of an angler, there's no better way to do that than to go fishing.

But that's a pretty soft, squishy answer to a hard question. And it doesn't cut much mustard with the people who make resource-management decisions. You don't gain much ground going before a congressional subcommittee and testifying that "I fish because it sure as hell beats working," or "because it makes me feel closer to God." In fact, both of those things may be absolutely true, but they are difficult to measure.

That's why it's necessary to quantify the value of sport fishing in economic terms. Personally I hate doing this, because I don't think of fishing in those terms; but dollars and cents seem to be the only language that bureaucrats and politicians are capable of understanding, so in order to make a case for the legitimacy of angling, we have to measure it in those terms. And that has been done.

The American Sportfishing Association, an organization supported by tackle and boat manufacturers and many angling groups, recently published a study showing that American anglers spent $8.7 billion to participate in marine recreational fishing in 1996, the most recent year for which figures were available. Those dollars rippled through all sectors of the US economy and generated a total economic impact of $25.1 billion, according to the ASA study.

The same study estimated that marine recreational fishing supported 288,000 full-time equivalent jobs and generated $1.24 billion in state and federal taxes in 1996. During that year, according to the US Fish and Wildlife Service, 9.4 million Americans aged sixteen and older fished in salt water. If children under sixteen are included, the total number of anglers exceeded 12 million.

Based on these figures, the ASA concluded that "while marine fishing is an enjoyable recreational sport for millions, it (also) has important economic benefits. Pursuit of the social, psychological, and physical benefits of sport fishing has given rise to an industry focused on supplying the goods and services necessary to meet angler demand and ensure satisfying recreational experiences . . . Several sectors of the economy, ranging from the sporting-goods industry to the travel and tourism sector, are to some degree dependent on sport fishing. In many small communities, sportfishing-related businesses are crucial to overall economic health and growth."

In our own state, marine sport fishermen spent more than $201 million in 1996, generating total economic output of more than $400 million and earnings of $108 million, and recreational fishing supported the equivalent of 4,605 full-time jobs. The state received $13 million in sales-tax revenues from marine sport fishing and the federal government received $11 million in taxes.

Now these figures may not quite equate with the economic impact of a Boeing or a Microsoft, but they are substantial. And historically, before pressures on our fisheries resulted in declining catches and declining participation, the economic impact of marine sport fishing in our state was undoubtedly much greater than it is now.

While we're on the subject of our own state, a 1991 US Fish & Wildlife Service study of Washington saltwater anglers found that 503,600 people spent 3,557,000 days fishing that year, an average of 7.1 days per angler. Not surprisingly, salmon accounted for the largest number of anglers—306,694—and the greatest number of days, 2,081,903.

I think it's kind of interesting that in the same survey, nearly 10,000 anglers reported they had fished for striped bass, which they might well have done, but I would guess their rate of success was pretty low since there are no striped bass in our state's waters. Yet the survey also revealed that striped-bass anglers in general have less education than other fishermen, with only slightly more than half having graduated from high school, so maybe that explains it.

Among the Washington anglers who fished for salmon in 1991, 72 percent were male and 28 percent were female. The same survey showed that 72 percent were married and 28 percent were single. Was this just coincidence, or could all of the male anglers have been married and all the females single? Or vice versa? The survey doesn't say, but it makes you wonder if there was something going on here besides fishing.

The survey showed that nearly a quarter of the salmon anglers had annual household incomes of more than fifty thousand dollars, and more than half were college graduates, so on the whole they appear to be a rather well-heeled, well-educated bunch. Maybe that helps explain why other studies have shown that the economic value of a sport-caught salmon or steelhead is much higher than that of one taken by commercial methods. In fact, the most recent studies estimate the value of a salmon or steelhead caught by an angler is anywhere from twelve to twenty-six times greater than a fish taken for commercial purposes.

They could be worth even more. In this state, you can buy a license to fish for salmon and other species in salt water for only eighteen dollars a year. Add another seventeen dollars and you can also fish for sea-run cutthroat trout. Add yet another eighteen dollars and you can fish for steelhead. If you break these figures down on a daily basis, you will find it costs only five cents a day in this state to fish for salmon and other saltwater species, and if you add both trout and steelhead, it costs only fourteen and a half cents a day. A politician once said that what this country needs is a good five-cent cigar. Well, we still don't have that, but we do have a five-cent-a-day fishing license, and if there's a greater bargain in existence, I don't know what it is.

Yet many people complain that fishing licenses cost too much, without realizing they probably spend more to gas up the car for a single day's fishing trip than they spend for a license that entitles them to fish every day of the year. If we raised the license fee to $365, which we ought to do, that would still mean a day's fishing would cost only a dollar—and that would still be an astounding bargain. It also would make recreational fishing even more valuable to the economy than it is now, and perhaps generate the funds that are so sorely needed to manage our fisheries properly. Of course, there would have to be a student discount for fishing licenses.

The whole point of all these figures is that marine recreational fishing in the United States is a big business, constantly getting bigger.

And on a worldwide scale, the US is only one slice of the pie; salt-water fishing is growing rapidly throughout North, Central, and South America, in Australia and New Zealand, in Africa and Europe, and even in the Red Sea and the Persian Gulf. It is an economic force to be reckoned with, and if, in the eyes of bureaucrats and politicians, economic value is tantamount to legitimacy, then sport fishing is very definitely a legitimate use of the world's oceans.

So, if you accept these conclusions, sport fishing has a justifiable claim to its share of the sea's resources for both quality-of-life and economic reasons. Yet there's still another reason, one perhaps even more practical than either of the others, and that is the potential of sport fishing to be a totally non-consumptive use. Sport fishing offers the opportunity to catch fish and release them, to let them go safely after their recreational purpose has been served, and many forms of marine fishing are moving rapidly in that direction. This is especially true of fly fishing, where catch-and-release is now the rule rather than the exception.

This is a classic case of being able to have your cake and eat it too. Using proper tackle and techniques, it is possible for anglers to hook, land, and release most saltwater species with little or no harm, thus subtracting nothing from the resource. Except possibly for whale watching, what other use of the oceans can make such a claim? Virtually every other use is, in some respect, either extractive or damaging or both.

Globally, we are now taking many more fish for food than the stocks can sustain. We also take oil and minerals from the sea floor, and once these are taken they are gone forever. We use the seas for commerce, which means oil spills and other forms of pollution. We fill in estuaries to make way for industry and in the process destroy the most productive biological habitats on the face of the earth. And the list goes on and on.

But recreational fishing has the potential, which is rapidly being realized, for taking nothing, for using the resource without using it up, for adding immeasurably to our quality of life and greatly to our economic health without extracting or damaging anything. To me, at least, that is a powerful moral imperative for its legitimacy, one that can't be matched by any other competing use of the seas.

In the future I assume that many of you will be in positions of responsibility for setting policy over our use of the seas and our management of their resources. As you face the difficult task of weighing all the competing demands for these resources, I hope you will remember these arguments for sport fishing as a legitimate use— not necessarily to the exclusion of others, but at least as an equal among many.

And when all the economic and practical criteria have been evaluated and applied, I would also urge you to remember what fishing means to the individual angler, the one who goes out day after day in all kinds of weather searching for an experience that cannot be obtained in any other way. For the thin line that connects an angler to a fish is ultimately like an electric wire, a wire that carries a magical current momentarily joining two very different beings. For the fisherman, that connection provides a brief glimpse into the world of an alien creature, a wild thing, a thing of beauty, strength, and instincts completely different from our own. It joins us with nature in a thrilling way that nothing else ever could, and changes us in ways we can never completely understand or fully explain, even to ourselves.

Perhaps, in the final analysis, fishing is simply our way of reaching out to the universe. I hope we will always have the opportunity to do that.

THE SOPHISTICATED ANGLER'S TEST (SAT)

TESTS ARE usually serious matters. If you do well, they might help you get into the college of your choice, or maybe land a job. This one, however, is mostly just for fun, though it *will* actually test your fly-fishing knowledge. You'll have a pretty good idea how well you did when you finish, so you don't even have to keep score unless you want to.

If you don't do very well, it's probably time you started getting out on the water a little more to sharpen your fly-fishing knowledge and skills, because that's where you learn the most. It also wouldn't hurt to read a few more fly-fishing books.

All the test questions are multiple-choice. Each question has at least one genuine actual correct answer, more or less, although in a few cases there might be more than one correct answer. This means that even if you just choose answers randomly, you should be able to get at least 25 percent right. No fair asking Alexa or Siri or another one of those digital voices, though. Looking things up on Google or Wikipedia is equally verboten. Use your head; that's why you have one.

If you decide to write down your answers, please do it on a separate sheet of paper. You wouldn't want to mess up this splendid book.

You'll find the real answers at the end of each test category so you can see how you did.

There are six categories with ten questions in each. If you're keeping score, award yourself a single point for each correct answer. There's also one trick question worth an extra point (total of two), and one extra-credit question, also worth two points. That means sixty-two is the top score possible.

Ready? Here we go:

Fly Fishing History:

1. What early angler said: "Who has not seen the scarus rise, decoyed and killed by fraudful flies"?
   a. Claudius Aelianus   b. Juliana Berners
   c. Martial   d. What the hell is a scarus?

2. What early angler cautioned fishermen to "break no man's hedges in going about your sports, nor open any man's gates without shutting them again"?
   a. Juliana Berners   b. Izaak Walton
   c. Charles Cotton   d. Ernest Schwiebert

3. He is generally credited with making the first six-strip, split-bamboo fly rod in America:
   a. Hiram Leonard   b. Fred Devine
   c. C. F. Orvis   d. Samuel Phillippe

4. During the late nineteenth and early twentieth centuries, he wrote many influential letters and "little talks on fly fishing" for *Forest and Stream* and the British *Fishing Gazette*:
   a. George LaBranche   b. Frederick Halford
   c. J. D. Mottram   d. Theodore Gordon

5. He is generally credited with developing nymph fishing:
   a. Frank Sawyer   b. Ernest Schwiebert
   c. G. E. M. Skues   d. Ray Bergman

6. He was one of the leaders in the drive to establish modern fly-line standards:
   a. Jim Green
   b. Myron Gregory
   c. Marvin Hedge
   d. Leon Chandler

7. The first conclave of what was then known as the Federation of Fly Fishers was held in:
   a. Sun Valley, Idaho
   b. Jackson Hole, Wyoming
   c. West Yellowstone, Montana
   d. Eugene, Oregon

8. Who was first president of the Federation of Fly Fishers?
   a. Ernest Schwiebert
   b. Lee Wulff
   c. Ted Trueblood
   d. Gene Anderegg

9. He is generally credited with inventing the process of impregnating bamboo fly rods with Bakelite phenolic resin:
   a. Hiram Leonard
   b. E. F. Payne
   c. Wes Jordan
   d. Lew Stoner

10. In 1991, outdoor humorist Ed Zern eulogized a great fly fisher in these words: "We salute this pioneer, this explorer, this adventurer, this innovator, this artist, this conservationist, this film maker, this author, this realist, this defender of sport's best traditions, this iconoclast of obsolete traditions, and above all, this great American sportsman." Who was he talking about?
    a. Lefty Kreh
    b. Lee Wulff
    c. Joe Brooks
    d. Edward R. Hewitt

Answers: (1) c (2) a (3) d (4) d (5) c (6) b (7) d (8) d (9) c (10) b

Fly Fishing Literature:
1. When Izaak Walton wrote *The Compleat Angler*, he borrowed liberally from the work of this person:
   a. Ernest Schwiebert
   b. Dame Juliana Berners
   c. Thaddeus Norris
   d. William Samuel

2. Author of *Days and Nights of Salmon Fishing in the Tweed*:
    a. George M. Kelson   b. Jock Scott
    c. Anthony Netboy   d. William Scrope

3. Nineteenth-century British author Henry Cholmondeley-Pennell wrote several seminal works on fishing. If you wanted to ask a librarian to find one, you'd need to know how the British pronounce "Cholmondeley":
    a. C'mon Dolly   b. Chum-Lee
    c. Chomon-delay   d. Schwiebert

4. He/she was author of *Minor Tactics of the Chalk Stream*:
    a. G. E. M. Skues   b. Frederic Halford
    c. Theodore Gordon   d. Mary Orvis Marbury

5. Author of *Fishing for Fun and to Wash Your Soul*:
    a. Billy Graham   b. Jimmy Carter
    c. Odell Shepherd   d. Herbert Hoover

6. Author of *Thy Rod and Thy Creel*:
    a. Billy Graham   b. Jimmy Carter
    c. Odell Shepherd   d. Herbert Hoover

7. He was perhaps the only concert opera singer ever to write a fly-fishing book:
    a. Placido Domingo   b. Harry Plunket Greene
    c. Luciano Pavarotti   d. Jack Hemingway

8. His novel, *Pool and Rapid*, was republished posthumously:
    a. Philip Wylie   b. William Humphrey
    c. Roderick Haig-Brown   d. Ernest Schwiebert

9. Author of *The Essence of Fly Casting*:
    a. Joan Wulff   b. Lefty Kreh
    c. Jacqueline Knight   d. Mel Krieger

10. *Trout Madness* and *Trout Magic*, both classics, were written by an author who used the pseudonym Robert Traver. What was his real name?
    a. W. D. Wetherell   b. Zane Grey
    c. John Voelker   d. Ernest Schwiebert

Answers: (1) d (2) d (3) b (4) a (5) d (6) c (7) b (8) c (9) d (10) c

Fly Fishing Nomenclature:

1. "Albright Special"
    a. A fly pattern for use during the Albright hatch
    b. An item on the menu at Burger King
    c. A fly pattern utilizing hackle from the rare Rosey-nosed Albright
    d. A knot sometimes used to join fly line to backing

2. "Butt section"
    a. Surgical treatment for hemorrhoids
    b. The first section of a rod (i.e., the one with a grip)
    c. The passenger seat in a drift boat
    d. The last inch of a good cigar

3. "Strike indicator"
    a. Symptom of labor problems
    b. The thing you stare at if you're fishing a chironomid pupa imitation
    c. Cowbell attached to the end of your propped-up cane pole
    d. Gizmo used by the home-plate umpire to keep track of balls and strikes

4. "Forceps"
    a. One more than threeceps
    b. Gadget used to remove hooks from fishermen
    c. May the forceps be with you!
    d. Gadget used to remove hooks from fish

5. "Tippet"
   a. When you leave a smaller tip than usual
   b. The part of your leader attached to the fly
   c. A choice cut of sirloin
   d. The part of your leader that always breaks

6. "Tenkara"
   a. Japanese dish featuring octopus tentacles
   b. One more than ninekara
   c. A Macedonian way of catching fish
   d. None of the above

7. "Bimini twist"
   a. A knot you tie with your knees
   b. Popular Latin dance
   c. Bacardi and soda with a dash of lime
   d. Breakfast pastry

8. "Stripping guide"
   a. A guide who takes off all his or her clothes
   b. Guidebook for exotic dancers
   c. The first and largest guide on the butt section of a fly rod
   d. A guide who takes off all his or her clothes and yours too

9. "Solunar Tables"
   a. They're on page 112 of the instructions for Form 1040
   b. Do you believe in the tooth fairy?
   c. An app for your phone
   d. Ernest Schwiebert

10. What is a "bead head"?
    a. George W. Bush
    b. A tropical rock band
    c. Type of shampoo
    d. A fly with a plastic or metal bead inserted on the hook and
       tied in behind the eye

Answers: (1) d (2) b (3) b (4) d, or maybe b (5) b, or maybe d.(6) d (7) a (8) c, or maybe a or d (9) c (10) d

Fly Patterns:

1. "Gray Ghost" originator
   a. Megan Boyd
   b. Joe Bates
   c. Carrie Stevens
   d. Helen Shaw

2. "Adams" originator
   a. Theodore Gordon
   b. Leonard Halladay
   c. Charles Adams
   d. Ernest Schwiebert

3. Here's the dressing:
   Tail: Strips of mottled turkey feather
   Body: Gold flat tinsel or Mylar
   Underwing: Tan calf tail
   Overwing: Matched mottled turkey feathers
   Collar: Deer hair
   Head: Deer hair spun and trimmed short
   What's the name of the pattern?
   a. Humpy
   b. Rat-faced McDougal
   c. Muddler Minnow
   d. Tom Thumb

4. "Pheasant Tail Nymph" originator
   a. Frank Sawyer
   b. G. E. M. Skues
   c. Ernest Schwiebert
   d. Jim Quick

5. Here's the dressing:
   Tail: Several barbules of natural or dyed blue dun hackle
   Body: Stripped peacock quill
   Wing: Wood duck or dyed mallard, upright and divided
   Hackle: Natural or dyed blue dun
   What's the name of the pattern?
   a. Adams
   b. Blue-winged Olive
   c. Quill Gordon
   d. Dark Hendrickson

6. This New Zealand bird was nearly rendered extinct because its feathers were so popular for fly tying:
   - a. Kiwi
   - b. Pukeku
   - c. Kea
   - d. Matuka

7. The "Sofa Pillow" fly pattern is usually attributed to:
   - a. Cal Bird
   - b. George Grant
   - c. Bud Lilly
   - d. Pat Barnes

8. Here's the dressing:
   Hook: Size 2/0 to 6, weighted
   Thread: Yellow
   Eyes: Lead, placed atop hook so hook rides up. Eyes painted dark red with black pupils
   Tail: Chartreuse bucktail
   Wing: Yellow bucktail with gold Flashabou or Krystal Flash mixed in
   What's the name of the pattern (this is one of numerous different versions)?
   - a. Lefty's Deceiver
   - b. Argentine Blonde
   - c. Clouser Deep Minnow
   - d. Key Lime Pie

9. It started out as the Michigan Hopper until popularized by Joe Brooks, after which this fly became known as Joe's Hopper. Who was the originator?
   - a. Ernest Schwiebert
   - b. Art Winnie
   - c. Bill Huddleston
   - d. Leonard Halladay

10. Here's the dressing:
    Hook: Size 2 or 4
    Thread: Pink

Eyes: 1/8 bead chain on size 4 hook or 5/32 bead chain on size 2, placed atop hook so hook rides up
Tail: Pearl Mylar tubing with strands teased out
Body: Pearl Diamond Braid
What's the name of the pattern?

a. Crazy Charlie
b. Gotcha
c. Hoochy Caucci
d. Nacho

Answers: (1) c (2) b (3) c (4) a (5) c (6) d (7) d (8) c (9) b (10) b

Fly-rod Fish:

1. Taxonomists have reclassified the rainbow trout as *Oncorhynchus mykiss*. What was its scientific name before it was reclassified?
   a. *Salmo trutta*
   b. *Salmo Irideus*
   c. *Salmo Gairdneri*
   d. *Salmo Schwieberti*

2. This splendid gamefish has a lung-like organ that allows it to survive in poorly oxygenated water by rolling on the surface and taking in air. What is the fish?
   a. Permit
   b. Roosterfish
   c. Triggerfish
   d. Tarpon

3. What fish was named after a character in a Charles Dickens novel? **(Extra point if you can also name the novel.)**
   a. Copperfield rockfish
   b. Brown trout
   c. Dolly Varden
   d. Grayling

4. This gamefish is a member of the genus *Thymallus*:
   a. Grayling
   b. Whitefish
   c. Sheefish
   d. Bonefish

5. This gamefish, originally imported from the East Coast but now firmly established on the West Coast, is a member of the herring family. What is the fish?
   a. Tarpon
   b. Striped bass
   c. Bonita
   d. Shad

6. The kokanee is actually a landlocked species of this salmon:
   a. Atlantic
   b. Sockeye
   c. Chinook
   d. Chum

7. The so-called lake trout is actually a species of:
   a. Whitefish
   b. Char
   c. Montana grayling
   d. Northern pikeminnow

8. The Eastern brook trout has no:
   a. Teeth
   b. Adipose fin
   c. Scales
   d. Eyebrows

9. The caudal peduncle is:
   a. Your stepfather's brother
   b. Not to be mentioned in polite company
   c. The narrow part of a fish's body to which the tail attaches
   d. On the cover of the *Sports Illustrated* swimsuit issue

10. **(Warning! Trick question; correct answer worth two points.)** If you caught a specimen of *Eosalmo driftwoodensis,* where and when would you have been fishing?
    a. New Jersey in April
    b. Northern Idaho in the Pleistocene Era
    c. New Brunswick in August
    d. British Columbia about forty million years ago

Answers: (1) c (2) d (3) c; the novel was *Barnaby Rudge* (4) a (5) d (6) b (7) b (8) c (9) c, or maybe d (10) d. *E. driftwoodensis* is the earliest known trout-like fossil fish, believed a forerunner of modern salmon, grayling, and whitefish. It was discovered in British Columbia.

Entomology:

1. *Zygoptera*:
   a. Caddisflies
   b. A small automobile manufactured in Albania
   c. Damselflies
   d. Dragonflies

2. *Coleoptera*:
   a. Stoneflies
   b. Beetles
   c. An invasive examination of the human lower digestive tract
   d. Backswimmers

3. *Hymenoptera*:
   a. Ask your doctor
   b. Caddisflies
   c. Ants
   d. Beetles

4. *Ephemera*:
   a. A burrowing stonefly
   b. A burrowing caddisfly
   c. A burrowing mayfly
   d. A burrowing Republican

5. *Siphlonurus*:
   a. Mayfly
   b. Caddisfly
   c. Midge
   d. A sexually transmitted disease

6. *Crustacean*:
   a. Sowbug
   b. Freshwater shrimp
   c. Lobster
   d. All the above

7. Hellgrammite:
   a. Member of a California motorcycle gang
   b. Alderfly larva
   c. Dragonfly nymph
   d. Dobsonfly larva

8. *Diptera*:
   a. Chironomid
   b. Beetle
   c. You were inoculated for it when you were a kid
   d. Water flea

9. *Enallagma*:
   a. Dragonfly
   b. Damselfly
   c. Scud
   d. World War II German coding device

10. *Tricorythodes*:
   a. Small town in southern Greece
   b. Carnivorous dinosaur
   c. Tiny, hard-to-imitate mayfly
   d. Trout liver parasite

Answers: (1) d (2) b (3) c (4) c (5) a (6) d (7) d (8) a (9) b (10) c

So how'd you do? C'mon now, tell the truth. Nobody else will know. And there's nothing at stake here; the only reward for having done well is the self-assurance that you can walk into any fly shop in the country and be able to understand the conversation.

The only consequence for having not done well is, I hope, some motivation to do better.

PART III: LATE SEASON

"The season is ended. There was not enough of it; there never is."—Nick Lyons

THE PAST IS PROSE

THERE ARE times in every angler's life when circumstances make it impossible to go fishing—health issues, family or business matters, weather (most often), or other problems—and these are occasions when a good fishing book can save the day. My library, which I've already described in detail, has rescued many such days for me, and its books have helped me become a better, more observant fisherman on those days when it is possible to get away.

It's a funny thing about books, though; they age at the same pace we do. As I've grown older, so have my books, until now, when I look back, I'm amazed how long it has been since I first read some of them. But if they are still on my shelves, there must be reasons why I kept them—there were many I didn't—and in most cases I still remember those reasons. Just to make sure, though, I decided recently to revisit some of these old volumes. I'll tell you a little about them here just in case you missed them the first time around and might want to look for them now. I think all are still available if you search long enough, and some are worth the search.

Here they are:

The Philosophical Fisherman, by Harold Blaisdell (1969)

I was still a young, wet-behind-the-ears fisherman when I read this one and I've always had a nostalgic attachment to it, not because it's a great book—it isn't—but more, I think, because I liked its attitude. I remember being impressed by the author's admission that what he knew about fishing was far less than what he didn't know. I'd already read many books by people who seemed to think they knew just about everything there was to know about fishing, especially fly fishing, so it was refreshing to find someone who admitted otherwise. I also enjoyed Blaisdell's relaxed writing style and repeated assertion that there are more important things in life than fishing (although I'd be hard-pressed to name more than one or two).

One of the more amusing tales in Blaisdell's book is his account of President Dwight D. Eisenhower's visit to Rutland, Vermont, near Blaisdell's home. "Because Ike was a fisherman," he wrote, "arrangements were made for him to fish the headwaters of Furnace Brook. There is a federal trout hatchery situated on the banks of the stream, so it goes without saying that the 'arrangements' included a heavy stocking of large trout in the stretch which the President was to fish." The hatchery superintendent, Blaisdell's friend, asked him to help distribute the fish, which was done at night so the trout would be in position for Eisenhower to catch in the morning. "We stumbled around in the dark, spotting two-, three- and even four-pound rainbow along the stream, and it was well after midnight when the job was finished."

It was all for naught. "Needless to say, the President caught none of the hefty trout. They were fat, hatchery-reared slobs, and were undoubtedly terrified by the sudden transfer to a harsher environment [but] local fishermen fared considerably better after the big trout had become at least partially acclimated . . . Although I know for a fact that Ike never caught a single fish, much was written about his efforts to do so . . . Much was also made of the fact that the President . . . was a regular fellow when it came to fishing. This feeling was neither misplaced [n]or an exaggeration, for Ike charmed all those who made up the party with his unaffected warmth and geniality."

I remembered that story from the first time I read the book. But if I hadn't read the book nearly fifty years ago and had just now picked it up for the first time, I'd probably feel less disposed to like it. For one thing, it's not all about fly fishing. In fact, Blaisdell dwells at length on other fishing methods and talks about fishing for species I consider disagreeable. I guess I was more tolerant at the tender age when I first read the book, with opinions that were less entrenched. I also liked the book's title, and do still. I think every fisherman should be philosophical; in fact, I'm not certain it is possible to *be* an ardent fly fisher without being philosophical.

Going Fishing, by Negley Farson (1943)

My old friend Al Severeid gave me a copy of this book many years ago, saying it was one that should be in any fishing library. Somehow, though, I never got around to reading it until recently.

I shouldn't have waited. Farson was a gifted writer, and though he describes fishing now more than seventy-five years in the past, his prose wears well. He was a well-known correspondent for various newspapers, traveling widely around the world looking for stories. But he always had a fly rod near his side, and usually a bottle of strong spirits.

"This is just the story of some rods, and the places they take you to," he says. Some places! In entertaining, frequently eloquent style, Farson tells of fishing for stripers on the New Jersey shore, "things in the water" of Africa's Lake Victoria, sea trout in the Shetland and Hebrides Islands, bass in the Catskills, trout in the Caucasus and elsewhere, sticklebacks in the Gulf of Finland, mackerel off the coast of

Egypt, trout and Pacific salmon in British Columbia, sturgeon in the Black Sea, and rainbow trout in the shadow of an erupting volcano in Chile—an amazing angling menu by any measure. Most of his adventures took place when transportation was primitive and many waters were seldom visited.

Writing about Pacific salmon on Vancouver Island in the 1930s, Farson said: "Great green and purple rocked mountains; storm clouds pouring in from the Pacific; driving rain drenching the forests; forests of spruce, of cedar, of fir—thick as the hair on the back of a dog—a wind-twisted, crashing maelstrom. We could hear the thundering roar of the [river], sluicing down to the sea, its rapids milk-white, foaming, swift as a hydraulic jet. A wild day, even for British Columbia when the rains are on . . . I looked over the side. And saw the Red Host. Great, red, pale-eyed salmon stared up from its depths; an army passed, phantom-like, underneath. Weary, covered with sores, they shot in from their fight with the stream, rested, and then silently took up their pilgrimage again. Thousands and thousands of salmon, up from the sea, to spawn and then die."

Farson also could see the humor in every situation. He tells of a banner day of trout fishing in the Caucasus, then (1929) part of the Soviet Union. Later, while frying up some of his catch, he was momentarily distracted and the fish got "slightly crisp." Then he was visited by a Cossack "who informed me that his official status was Instructor in Communism." The Commie Cossack ate one of the crispy trout, "pronounced it marvelous, but said that I was a Capitalist because I had used a fly" to catch it.

Farson always had time for at least a wee dram when he was fishing. After a day of fly fishing for trout in Chile in 1937, he rendezvoused with two companions, a Scot and an Englishman, "who held the bottle out to me . . . 'Funny, isn't it,' smiled the Englishman as I wiped my lips, 'how damned *good* it tastes after a day like this! Nothing like the same taste in a city . . . .'"

But you didn't need a book to tell you that.

Squaretail, by Charles Kroll (1972)

It wouldn't be surprising if you missed this one. That's because it was published by a so-called "vanity press," where the author pays the publisher to produce the book instead of the other way around. Usually this happens after an author receives so many rejection slips from publishers he figures the only way his or her book will ever see the light of day is to pay to have it published. Vanity press books usually get little publicity and are generally ignored by reviewers, so they often go unnoticed.

In this case, it's difficult to believe *Squaretail* was rejected by established publishers because it was probably the most complete work on Eastern brook trout ever written to that time. True, it suffers a little from irregular punctuation, but who reads a book for its punctuation? The language, on the other hand, is as good or better than many works from publishing houses that actually pay authors for their work.

The book's foreword, by Robert J. Good, makes Charles Kroll, the author, sound larger than life: "Everything about him smacked of professionalism," Good wrote, "from the battered, weather-worn Stetson and Mucelin-stained vest down to the stream-worn Hardy Model Perfect. His special intenseness was evident in the angle of the half-cold cigar locked in set jaws between clenched teeth. The tenderness with which he held each trout as he studied its individual beauty before the release almost belied that intenseness, but made you aware of the man's devotion to the pursuit of the crimson-flecked denizens of these streams . . . It was only after the willows closed over his departing shadow that you fully realized that he walked with the aid of a cane." Who was that masked man, anyway?

Kroll might have needed a cane, but it sure didn't hobble his writing: "Small brooks meandering through northeastern cedar and tamarack swamps, where the water gliding beneath the overhanging boughs is the color of dark amber, hold fish whose forebears swam there 20,000 years ago—fish mantled with flowing shades of color, from olive through beige, soft blue and fawn into ivory, among the loveliest of their species." From that beginning, Kroll goes on to describe the brook trout's natural history—the "gems of creation," he calls them—their distribution across North America and introduction to South America, the types of water they inhabit (including anadromous runs of brook trout), fly patterns, and fishing tactics.

You probably could have gotten the same information in bits and pieces from a lot of other books at the time, but Kroll was perhaps the first to put it all together in a single volume. *Squaretail* was largely superseded twenty-five years later by Nick Karas's work on brook trout, but it still makes nostalgic reading about a time when brookies, and opportunities to fish for them, were far more widespread than they are now.

Where the Pools Are Bright and Deep, by Dana S. Lamb (1973)

Dana Lamb was a popular writer in the 1960s and early '70s, but who remembers him now? He wrote at least nine books, some published only in limited editions, and most were a series of brief, slice-of-life angling essays, with occasional detours into wingshooting. This one includes forty-one essays in 145 pages, about three and a half pages per essay. That makes it a book that's easy to pick up or put down as often as you like; no interminably long chapters here. It's also graced by the illustrations of Eldridge Hardie, one of the all-time great outdoor artists.

One of the first things that caught my eye in this book was its dedication: "In memory of a 19-year-old sergeant from Vermont, my great-uncle, Lewis Lamb. Accounted by his comrades in his native state's Eighth Regiment of Veteran Volunteers as 'noble, generous and brave,' he fell while fighting well at Cedar Creek at harvest time in 1864." I could identify with that; my great-grandfather, Sergeant Jonathan Butler of the Seventy-Eighth Illinois Volunteer Infantry, also fell at harvest time in 1864 at the battle of Jonesboro, Georgia. Although gravely wounded, he survived; otherwise I wouldn't be writing this.

But I digress. What makes this book—or any Dana Lamb book—so appealing is his serene, lyrical writing style. There's nothing heavy here, no how-to stuff, no pontificating or theorizing, just easy, relaxing stories, the kind best read in front of a winter fire, reminding readers of pleasant days past and the promise of more to come. Some samples:

From a piece called "New Brunswick Morning": "Here, where the passing salmon pause to rest beside the underwater rocks, calm and quietness prevail. But upriver, where around a bend unyielding cliffs stand guard to herd rebellious currents through a narrow gorge, the river snarls like a panther in a trap, its roaring carried by the wind across long miles of wilderness."

From "Going Out to Get the Mail": "Now, as with the family setter dog at heel he made this long familiar trip he thought of endless disappointing visits to the place as well; times in hopes, forever vain, of finding scented letters from a girl who never wrote or something from an editor besides rejection slips. Today there was no letter from his son; just appeals for contributions to what the writer, in each instance, called 'a worthy cause,' a statement from the Grange, an Orvis catalogue."

From "Season's End": "The leafy surface of the rich brown earth is dappled as the sunlight filters through the still-green leaves; the glade is resonant with joyous songs of birds. The robins, warblers, swallows and the summer yellowbirds are flocking up before they start their long flight south. The solitary angler's gaze pursues their fitful progress from the maples to the sycamores or out across the placid pool."

From "Well Anyway—Almost": ". . . An angler, with the passing years, will find his memories more flexible than facts. My recollections, happier by far than what is written in my conscientious day-to-day accounts, put dull statistics in the shade. That's why dust gathers

on the leather cover of the *Fishing Log* I've hidden way back underneath the eaves. Long, long ago, my diaries lay open on the table in
my den. On winter evenings, with my shorthair pointer and my glass
of Highland Malt, I'd watch the flaming cedar logs chase shadows up
the paneled walls and think about the salmon rivers that I loved."

Good words, those. I could read them all winter.

In Trout Country, edited by Peter Corodimas (1971)

This was published as a *Sports Illustrated* book back in the days
when that magazine still considered fishing a sport. The dust jacket
illustration—an angler carrying a creel—clearly dates it to a time
when the notion of catch-and-release was still in its infancy.

In Trout Country is an anthology, a collection of twenty-seven stories about trout fishing. The editor, Peter Corodimas, a college English professor, chose well, selecting a rich variety of reading. He also
wrote well, if the book's introduction is an indication. Extolling the
virtues of the trout that have inspired so many literary works, Corodimas cites William Butler Yeats' famous poem, "The Song of Wandering Aengus." It describes, he says, "a Celtic god who hooks a berry
to a thread, drops it into a stream, and catches 'a little silver trout.'
Later, the trout changes into 'a glimmering girl / With apple blossom
in her hair.'" To understand "how idealized the trout has become,"
Corodimas says, "try substituting another fish for Yeats' trout. A little
silver shiner? A little yellow perch? A little green pike? A little copper
bass?" You get the point. "By allying himself with the trout, the trout
fisherman has prospered beyond his wildest dreams; indeed, no other
fisherman has made out half so well." He means the trout fisherman
has prospered in literature, and proves his case with the selections in
this book. But while all the tales in this book are about trout—fair
warning—not all the trout are caught on flies.

A few stories are classics—Richard Brautigan's memorable yarn
about a wrecking yard with sections of used trout stream for sale,

Paul O'Neil's "In Praise of Trout—And Also Me," Ed Zern's hilarious "Something Was Fishy about Stonehenge," and Robert Traver's "The Intruder" (there are two Traver stories in this collection, even though his name was misspelled once in the table of contents). Inevitably, Hemingway's "Big Two-Hearted River" is here, too. Other well-known angling writers—R. Palmer Baker, Jr., Dana Lamb, Philip Wylie, R. D. Blackmore, Edward Weeks, and Corey Ford—also are represented.

Some of these writers, and many others, also are to be found in another anthology, *Fisherman's Bounty,* compiled by Nick Lyons and published a year before *In Trout Country*. But Lyons's book covers more fish (salmon, steelhead, carp, bass, muskellunge, and saltwater species), more fishing methods, and a greater span of time. Surprisingly, there isn't much overlap between the two books; Traver's "The Intruder" and R. D. Blackmore's "Crocker's Hole" are the only stories that appear in both.

There's lots of good reading in these two volumes, and although both have been around for going on fifty years, they remain as fresh and relevant as ever. They should be required reading for every angler, especially those just beginning to wade the sacred waters of angling literature.

Fresh Waters, by Edward Weeks (1968)

I first read this book many years ago and remembered it fondly, but when I picked it up recently and started reading it again I began to wonder why. The author, Edward Weeks, had a distinguished career as editor of the Atlantic Monthly Press and *Atlantic Monthly* magazine, publishing writers such as Ernest Hemingway and classic titles such as *Mutiny on the Bounty*. But he was in his forties before he started fishing and the first chapters of this book are mostly about his early experiences with bamboo rods and gut leaders, using worms and plugs to fish for pickerel, perch, and other unglamorous species—the sort of things most anglers do when they're young and just getting started. Weeks did them in middle age and these early chapters are a bit like looking at somebody's childhood photo album.

I kept reading, though, and about halfway through the book, after Weeks graduated to fly fishing for trout, salmon, steelhead, and other more challenging species, I began to rediscover why I liked the book so much on first reading. On periodic trips abroad, scouting for new writers or unpublished manuscripts, Weeks always took a fly rod and was ever on the lookout for fishing opportunities. He found them in Uzbekistan, where he "caught nothing but friends"; in what was then Yugoslavia; and repeatedly on the chalk streams of England, chronicling his adventures in rich prose. His description of St. James Street in London would have made Ernest Schwiebert jealous:

"Here is every delight but one to please the male: wine from Berry Brothers, whose cellars deep under the pavement were first reinforced to support the coronation coaches of Charles II; hats from Lock's, whose shop has been swept but otherwise unchanged from the days they were shaping a cocked hat for Lord Nelson; from Prunier's delectable bisque homard and Dover sole; from Webley's a fowling piece or rifle to match your build, and at the upper level, those clubs, Boodle's and White's, Brooks's and Pratt's, whose banter and decorum are a perpetual surprise to the American visitor. Around the lower end of St. James's on Pall Mall and across from the Palace is Hardy's Fishing . . . the cornucopia of English angling."

Weeks also dropped enough names to make Schwiebert blush, but never ostentatiously. He fished the Klamath with Clark Van Fleet, author of the classic *Steelhead to a Fly,* and the Gold River on Vancouver Island with Roderick Haig-Brown. He made friends with and wrote about Dr. Lauren Donaldson, pioneering University of Washington fisheries professor and my old friend. He also was a frequent visitor at Salmon Brook Camp on the Miramichi in New Brunswick, which meant nothing to me when I first read about it years ago but later became my base for fishing that great river. Weeks's guide way back then was a relative of the man who much later guided me.

OK, you say, maybe you just had to be there to appreciate all this. But with Weeks, you *are* there, sharing his love for the people, the places, and most of all for the fishing. Reading about fly fishing doesn't get much better than this. It's all right if you choose to skip the opening chapters and start in, say, at about Chapter 8.

Trout at Taupo, by O. S. Hintz
(new and enlarged edition, 1964)

What's a book from New Zealand doing on this list of old tomes? Well, if ever you needed proof that fly fishers speak a universal language and share common experiences, you'll find it here. *Trout at Taupo*, like most other books listed here, describes fishing that may not exist anymore, or, if it does exist, is not the same. Yet the book makes it abundantly clear that the attitudes, spirits, vocabularies, practices, and humor of fly fishers hardly ever change.

O. S. Hintz's full name was Orton Sutherland Hintz, which probably explains why he always went by the nickname "Budge" (which also might have had to do with his physical stature). He was editor of the *New Zealand Herald*, and like another editor I know, he sought solace and escape through fishing—in his case, on the bountiful waters of Lake Taupo and its numerous tributaries.

I'd heard of this book somewhere and was surprised to find a copy in the catacombs of a secondhand bookstore near Seattle's Pioneer Square. It still had the original price written on the inside cover—$2—so I bought it on the spot. How could I not? I hadn't yet been to New Zealand when I bought it, but once I read it I knew I had to go. Several years later the opportunity came, and thanks to Hintz I had a good idea what to expect when I got there.

Hintz recites native Maori legends about the restless volcanic past of the mountains surrounding the great inland sea of Lake Taupo and provides a good history of the introduction of trout to the lake. He describes the fishing tactics and flies used in the lake and the rivers that flow into it, and rhapsodizes over the many scenic attractions of the countryside. But he's at his best when telling fishing stories, including many that will make you smile and others that will make you laugh out loud.

One thing I gleaned from my first reading of this book was a desire to fish the little Waitahanui, Hintz's favorite Taupo stream—he devotes an entire chapter to it—and I headed there soon after I arrived in New Zealand on my second trip. His description was right on the nose, and the Waitahanui greeted me generously, just as the Kiwi fishermen did.

It's easy to like Budge Hintz and wish he was your fishing buddy, but there are a few things in this book that illustrate how much things have changed since it was written—and we're not just talking about the fishing. One change is that catch-and-release had yet to make its way to New Zealand when Hintz was fishing Taupo, and nearly every fish caught in these pages was killed. Another is that every fish was either a "he" or a "him"; as far as Hintz was concerned, there were apparently no females. Yet another is that a lot of cigarettes get smoked in Hintz's prose. Thank goodness all those things have changed.

Others, thankfully, have not. "I have the faint hope that I may be writing for a wider public," Hintz says, "that this book will find its way into the hands of anglers in older lands and that some chance passage or anecdote will persuade them to pack bags, organize passports, gather up their favourite rods and tackle, and set forth across the world to a small country of insular but warm-hearted people who will bid them welcome cordially."

That's how they welcomed me. I hope it may happen to you.

Hintz went on to write a later companion volume, *Fisherman's Paradise*, that's just as pleasant to read as this one. But that's another book and another story.

CHERNOBYL TOMATO

IT'S CALLED Lone Lake, but don't let the name fool you—it's anything but lonely. There are lots of homes around it, many with nice lawns extending down to the shore. There are also several farms where cows, horses, and alpacas graze. The lake is always busy with fishermen and boaters, and swimmers in season. It's far from a wilderness angling venue, yet for me Lone Lake has two important virtues: It holds rainbow trout, some of large size, and it's only about fifteen minutes from my home. That makes it a handy place to drop in for a few hours of fishing.

That's what I was doing one spring afternoon when large chironomids were hatching and trout were nosing through the surface to take them. I tied on a chironomid pupa imitation to match the naturals and cast to a subtle rise tight against the weeds where big trout often cruise. I gave the fly a little twitch, felt immediate resistance, set the hook—and this *THING* began moving ponderously toward the center of the lake, taking my fly line with it. It wasn't the swift run of a rainbow, but more of a strong, slow, steady pull, as if I'd hooked a power lawnmower.

Muskrat? Beaver? Somebody's escaped pet alligator?

None of the above. When the thing finally came to the surface, I saw I had hooked a hugely fat, hideously ugly grass carp, *Ctenopharyngodon idella*. When I saw how big it was I knew I'd have to handle it carefully on the light tackle I was using.

The carp made several short, strong runs, taking line each time, then headed for the bottom, where it grubbed around like a pig rooting through a landfill. After about ten minutes of this it finally returned to the surface, rolled onto its fat side, and came obligingly to my boat.

It was built like a garbage bag, which made it difficult to estimate its weight, but my guess was somewhere between five and ten pounds. Grass carp are supposed to be vegetarians, but this one obviously hadn't gotten the memo; it had clamped down hard on my chironomid pupa imitation, which was stuck firmly in one of its thick, disgusting lips. I didn't want to touch the ugly thing, but I did want my fly back, so I reached out and managed to twist the barbless hook free without even touching the fish. I watched the carp swim slowly away, then threw up.

Just kidding. I didn't really throw up. I sure thought about it, though.

It wasn't my intention, but I had just proven grass carp can be taken on an artificial fly. Keep that in mind as you continue reading.

How the carp got there is an interesting story. Lone Lake has long been a popular place for people to empty their goldfish bowls, and God alone knows what all is swimming around out there. At some point, one of those goldfish bowls contained Brazilian elodea, a fast-growing invasive weed that quickly gained a foothold in the lake. It spread so rapidly that within a few years vast areas of the lake became clogged with weed and were no longer usable for fishing, swimming, boating, or anything else. The lake was on the verge of becoming a marsh, the next-to-last stage before it would become a meadow. Something had to be done to stop the weed's spread, and the Lone Lake Homeowners Association, the county government, and several local fly-fishing clubs banded together to seek a solution.

Once nuclear weapons were ruled out, the groups decided to treat the lake with an herbicide that kills Brazilian elodea but is harmless to fish and insects. The results were immediate and dramatic: Great clots of dead weed floated to the surface and washed ashore, and suddenly all of Lone Lake was again open for fishing, swimming, and boating.

The effects of the herbicide were only temporary, however. Something more was needed to keep the weed from coming back. Grass carp had been used for this purpose in other settings, with mixed results, but they appeared to offer the most promise, so the county applied for a state permit to plant sterilized *Ctenopharyngodon idella* in Lone Lake. State fisheries managers understandably weren't thrilled at the idea of introducing a new exotic species, even if the carp were sterilized, and denied the permit. Twice more the county applied, and finally, in the absence of any other remedy, the state reluctantly approved.

The next step was to figure out how many carp should be planted. The available scientific literature was sketchy, lacking any established stocking formula, but biologists eventually came up with a figure of eight fish per acre. Since Lone Lake has 101 surface acres, that meant 808 carp.

I don't know where they got the carp—Mars, maybe, or some equally alien venue—but 808 sterilized grass carp were planted in Lone Lake in the spring of 2007. At the time of planting, they averaged about twelve inches in length, but they can live up to ten years and reach weights of forty pounds under optimal grazing conditions.

The carp wasted no time doing what they were supposed to do, chomping every weed in sight. Periodic sampling of the lake showed steadily declining levels of aquatic vegetation. In fact, after a couple of years, sampling showed no aquatic vegetation whatever. That explained why anglers had begun to notice declining insect hatches; there was no longer any aquatic weed habitat for insects to breed in or feed in. It also explained why the trout in Lone Lake were beginning to look skinny.

Worse was to come. Removal of the aquatic vegetation allowed water-borne nutrients to become concentrated in blue-green algae, resulting in thick blooms toxic enough to kill house pets.

It was obvious things had gotten seriously out of whack, as often seems to happen when one exotic species is used to try to control another. Something had to be done to reduce the population of super-efficient carp in order to restore a balance between weed growth and carp numbers; otherwise it probably wouldn't be long before *Cteno-pharyngodon idella* started hungrily eyeing the well-kept lawns of lakeside residents.

How do you thin a population of grass carp? Easy: You just ask anglers to catch them. State fisheries managers invited members of the Whidbey Island and Evergreen Fly Fishing Clubs to join in a special carp-fishing season with a goal of reducing the carp population by about 160 fish.

But there was a catch: To reduce impacts on non-target fish species, such as trout, carp anglers would be required to use "barbless hooks baited with baits attractive only to grass carp. These include lettuce, spinach, alfalfa, sunflower sprouts, grass clippings, cherry tomatoes, and fresh fruit."

That's an actual quote. I'm not making this stuff up.

Why anyone thought fly fishers would be interested in a fishery requiring the use of fruits and vegetables for bait is beyond me, especially when I knew from recent experience that grass carp could be taken on an artificial fly. If they'd take a chironomid imitation, why not imitation fruits and vegetables?

That idea, however, apparently was never considered, and as this is being written the special fruits-and-vegetables-only carp season has been under way for several months. From what I hear, it's not going very well. Not very many anglers have participated and not very many carp have been caught, even though various combinations of garden produce and ripe fruit have been employed. One determined local fly fisherman, obviously not a purist, even tried chumming with grass clippings.

Too bad. Just think what might have been: If anglers had been allowed to use artificials, every fly tyer in the state would have descended on Lone Lake, anxious to try his or her own hand-crafted fruit and vegetable imitations. Imagine the new flies we'd all be talking about: Lefty's Lettuce. Skykomish Sunripe. Woolly Rutabaga. Sparse Grape Hackle.

The carp wouldn't have had a chance. By now the weeds would be growing back in Lone Lake, the bugs would be hatching again, and the literature of fly fishing would have a whole new genre of patterns to celebrate: Beet-head Nymph. Crazy Chardlie. Eggplant-sucking Leech. Kale Morning Dun. Chernobyl Tomato.

"GET THEM BACK ALIVE!"

AFTER A ten-year hiatus, I returned to Christmas Island a third time. The first thing I noticed was the sign about no tipping was still missing from the dining room at the Captain Cook Hotel. That told me the guides had finally gotten their priorities in order, and this time I wasn't planning to write anything about them; I was there just to fish and have fun. My son, Randy, was with me, along with my old friend Dave Draheim, a veteran of my first trip to Christmas, and his son, Chris.

This would be Randy's first exposure to bonefishing, so when we drew our guide assignments for the first day of fishing I made sure he was paired with the more experienced of the two assigned to us. His name was Neemia and he was a thirteen-year veteran.

It was a good choice. Under Neemia's tutelage, Randy landed four bonefish that morning, including one Neemia estimated at about seven pounds. Not a bad start!

After lunch we traded guides so I had a chance to get acquainted with Neemia, who turned out to be probably the most low-key guide I'd had at Christmas Island. He also spoke better English than most of the other guides. When I blew shots at the first seven or eight fish we saw—a performance I attributed to chronic rustiness—he also displayed admirable patience. Eventually I was able to salvage a little self-respect when I connected with a big fish that ran far into the backing, not once but four times, before I managed to bring it to hand. Neemia estimated that one also weighed seven pounds—maybe that was his favorite number. I didn't think it was quite that big, but it was still big enough to please me.

Bad weather kept our catch to a minimum the next couple of days, but Neemia earned his keep by spotting fish I couldn't see in the poor light and heavy chop. I hooked several, including a five-pounder that ran over the edge of a flat and fouled my line on a coral head. Neemia dashed after it, freed the line, and I got the fish.

After several days of fishing with guides, Randy wanted to try his luck without one, so he went alone while I went with Neemia again. We both had a good day— for me, seventeen fish hooked and fourteen landed, including another five-pounder; for Randy, fourteen hooked and eight landed, including a grand fish of eight pounds or more, with photographic evidence to prove it. I was highly pleased at the way he seemed to be taking to this fishing. Maybe it was the genes.

Dave and Chris, fishing with different guides, weren't doing as well, although one day Chris hooked a big, angry bonefish that spooled him. That also was the day we came in from fishing and found our truck stuck up to the axles in muck. Two of the guides were sitting on the hood, hoping their weight would give the truck more traction; they didn't realize the drive wheels were in back. We acquainted them with the facts of truck life and several of us piled into the back while everyone else got behind to push, and the truck finally broke free. I suppose it was too much to expect Christmas Island fishing guides would be automotive experts, too.

It's a long way from Christmas Island in the Pacific to South Andros Island in the Bahamas, but that was my next bonefishing destination, at a resort called Andros South (don't ask me why the owners turned the island's name around). Randy was again with me along with three friends, Keith Robbins, Steve Sunich, and Dave Schorsch.

Most of the fishing at South Andros was in a labyrinth of mangrove-lined saltwater creeks and bays dividing the southern part of the island from the rest of it. Flats boats, each carrying a pair of anglers and a guide, were used for transportation and for most of the fishing, due to limited wading opportunities. That meant Randy and I would have to take turns fishing from the bow of the flats boat, which also meant we'd have only half the fishing time we'd had at Christmas Island.

The guides were experienced and competent, save one who had the worst attitude of any guide I've met. If he'd ever known fishing is supposed to be fun he'd obviously forgotten it, and he spent most of his time criticizing and pressing us to do things his way and do them better and faster. Fortunately, guides were rotated daily, so Randy and I had to suffer his company only once. The other guides were uniformly friendly, cordial, and helpful.

We spent two days fishing in weather ranging from marginal to impossible, with minimal results. The third day dawned equally unpromising, with continued wind and overcast, but our guide that day was a laid-back fellow named Charlie who took us up Deep Creek and poled around the lee edges of the mangroves, searching for places we might be able to see fish and cast to them. Randy and I each got a pair of bones, though nothing larger than three pounds. We ended up wading a flat we had fished the day before in horrible weather. This time we could see things better and I managed to zero in on a fair number of fish, but most fled before I could get within casting range. Charlie stayed with Randy and caught a pair of bones on a rod I loaned him so he also could fish. Then he teamed up with me and pointed out several fish, but I managed to blow every opportunity, including almost literally bouncing my fly off the head of one of the biggest bonefish I'd ever seen. Randy, fishing alone, landed a single two-pounder.

The next day was spent with the ill-tempered guide mentioned previously, so the less said about it, the better—except, with gallant help from Randy, I did land a single big bonefish. It ran into a tangle of mangroves and wrapped my line around a root as thick as a firehose, but Randy jumped in, waded into the tangled roots, freed the line, and I got the fish. The ill-tempered guide estimated its weight at five pounds; I'd have said six. Randy took its photo and showed it to our friends back at the lodge; they all thought it would have weighed eight pounds.

They were good friends.

Long overdue sunny and calm weather greeted us on our fifth day. With a guide named Norman at the helm, we ran through saltwater creeks all the way to the open sea on the west side of the island, where we encountered a mysterious thicket of sea haze that blotted out the horizon between sea and sky. It looked as if we were about to disappear into the Bermuda Triangle, never to be seen again, when Norman turned back toward the island and we entered a large, shallow bay.

Norman was a great guide, very helpful, and put us into places where we saw *many* bonefish—singles, doubles, sometimes a whole posse or more. We each landed eight, including the biggest bonefish I've ever caught. Randy saw it first and pointed it out, I covered it with a cast from the bow. The fish took immediately and ripped off at least one hundred yards of backing, and after a long fight that left me weary from reeling, I brought it alongside. Randy immortalized it with his camera, Norman said it was a good ten pounds, and I didn't argue. It was the kind of day, and the kind of fishing, we'd hoped to find in the Bahamas.

On our last day we requested Charlie for our guide because he and Randy had gotten along so well when we fished with him earlier. The morning was mostly clear with a gentle breeze. We ran up Little Creek and ended up poling apparently endless flats somewhere in the maze of interior waterways. The weather slowly deteriorated, however, and by afternoon the wind was twenty knots and we were being hit with sporadic rain showers. Nevertheless, Randy and I each managed to score a single bonefish, both at the same time—the first double-header we'd had. One of us—I don't remember which—had hooked a fish and stepped off the bow to play it while the other got up on the bow, made a cast, and hooked the second fish.

On our way back we saw some other fish and I hooked and landed one. Randy mounted the bow to take his turn, and that gave me a chance to tell Charlie there was a question I wanted to ask him. "I'm serious about this," I said, "so don't laugh." He grinned hugely and told me to go ahead. I said we'd heard he was a deacon in the local Baptist church, and he nodded affirmation. "OK, then, my question is: When you're out fishing like this, do you ever pray that your clients will catch fish?"

His grin got even wider; then he burst into laughter. "No, mon," he said finally. "I just pray that I get them back alive."

My kind of guide.

We gave Charlie our usual daily tips, but then I added $20 "for the collection plate at your church." His face lit up like a Christmas tree.

Two years later Randy and I made yet another pilgrimage to Christmas Island, this time just the two of us. By then macular degeneration, a common ailment of old age, had cost me most of the sight in one eye, so I wasn't sure I'd still be able to see bonefish as well as I could when younger.

It didn't take long to find out. The weather on our first day wasn't especially conducive to seeing fish, but it was good enough for me to realize I *couldn't* see them—at least, not like I always had. My guide, Naurio, a veteran of more than twenty years, had good vision, however, so his eyes became my eyes. He would see a fish and tell me where and how far to cast, and with his help I hooked thirteen bones that morning. Randy went with him in the afternoon and got only a single fish, but it was a big one, seven or eight pounds. Fishing the afternoon by myself, I saw and caught nothing.

Next day I had a different guide, this one with only three years' experience. He was pleasant and could spot fish fairly well, but it was obvious he still had much to learn. We saw lots of fish—or rather, the guide saw them—but they didn't seem in a taking mood. I lost one and hooked another the guide said would have gone four pounds, but he bungled the landing and broke off the fish. He also insisted on tying knots for me, although I could still see well enough to do that, and two of his knots failed on other fish.

We finally reached a spot in the main lagoon where we could wade along a bar and see bonefish coming in from both sides—even I could see them. I landed three in quick succession and lost a very large fish when the hook pulled out. Then the outrigger pulled up with Naurio and Randy aboard. I told the guide to yell at them to go away, but Naurio, the senior guide, insisted it was time for us to go, so we had to leave the best setup I'd seen—wind and light at our backs, lots of fish, and I could *see* them. Instead, we motored through the maze of islets known as Y Site and got onto a flat where there was no water— the tide had gone out—and trudged for what seemed like miles until we reached an edge where occasional fish were cruising past in deep water. By then I was tired and my back ached, but I still managed to land two more small bonefish and three small trevally.

By the next day my backache had escalated into debilitating spasms around the site of an old fracture, so while Randy went with the guides I climbed into the back of the truck, stretched out, and tried vainly to sleep, bothered not only by pain but also the irony of how critical I'd been of the guides for napping in the truck on my first trip to Christmas Island. Now I was trying to do it myself.

That night Randy came to the rescue. An Eagle Scout with advanced first-aid training, he always carries what appears to be a portable pharmacy. It provided a variety of pills, rubs, ointments, and other remedies that eventually drove the spasms away, and for the next few days he kept me dosed up so that I was able to resume fishing. For that I was most grateful, especially since my ailments had forced me to conclude this would probably have to be my last bonefishing trip and I'd better make the best of it.

Next day we had a new guide who told us his name was Mike, probably so we wouldn't massacre the pronunciation of his real name. He'd been guiding twenty-five years and knew his stuff. He also brought with him a young guide-in-training whose name was such a complicated assemblage of vowels it looked like it had been encrypted. We never did learn how to spell or pronounce it.

Mike proved very good at seeing fish in less-than-optimal conditions, and with him calling the shots I hooked nine fish in the morning, including a couple around four pounds each. One was tailing in a small circle and I cast five or six times before it finally saw the fly and took it. After I landed it, Mike hugged me and said, "You a good fisherman."

But he probably says that to all his customers.

In the afternoon I fished with the trainee. He was very young—around twenty, I guessed—but very friendly and accommodating. He also was totally lacking equipment. He waded barefoot, and although he had tough, leathery feet from a lifetime of going barefoot, he still could not escape cutting and scraping his feet on the sharp coral. The soles of his feet were crisscrossed with angry wounds which must have been extremely uncomfortable, but he never complained or slowed down. He also had no Polaroid glasses and had to rely on his own unaided vision to see fish, which he did amazingly well under the circumstances, although I don't remember if we caught any.

Randy generously offered to accompany the trainee next morning and I went with Mike. At a place called Lone Palm I hooked sixteen bonefish in less than two hours but landed only nine. Most of the others just came unpinned. Then I hooked a very large bonefish that started toward New Zealand and kept running until the tippet knot ultimately failed. Later I hooked and landed another good fish that Mike estimated at six pounds. I would have said five.

Randy hadn't had much action with the trainee, so we swapped guides in the afternoon. I hooked another very large bonefish that ran a long way before it finally straightened the hook and went on its merry way. That was all.

Our last day was perfect, with bright sunshine and only a little wind. I was with the trainee when I hooked a fish that quickly escaped when the tippet knot failed—a knot the trainee had tied. I remembered Randy had said he'd lost three fish the day before because of the trainee's badly tied knots, so I told the youngster I'd tie on the next fly. Eager to learn, he watched closely as I did so. Before the day was over he asked me twice more to demonstrate the knot until he finally seemed to have it down and was tying it himself. After that his knots held.

After lunch we went to a flat I remembered fishing on an earlier trip. This time I was with Mike, who could usually see fish if there were any to be seen. When I told him I thought I saw one he hadn't sighted, he looked around wildly and asked "where?" Instead of replying, I cast to the fish, hooked it, and landed it. "Don't ever do that again!" Mike said. "Only the guide is supposed to see fish!" He was kidding and we both laughed, but afterward I noticed a little change in his attitude; he was more respectful of someone who could at least occasionally see fish, even with only one eye.

We finished the day on Paris Flat, another place I remembered fondly from earlier visits. For more than two hours we stayed in the same spot near the edge of the snow-white flat and watched fish approach in growing numbers. Most were small, but I landed one that was a good five pounds—my estimate, not Mike's. For the day I hooked eighteen and landed twelve, while Randy landed thirteen, one of his best days.

When it was time to head back, Mike and the trainee both thanked us respectfully and said it was their honor to have been our guides. We assured them the thanks and the honor were ours. In four trips to Christmas Island I'd fished with guides who were good and others who were mediocre, but Mike surely was high on the list of the good ones. His young sidekick was very green with much to learn, but he was so likeable, enthusiastic, and eager that I predicted a bright future for him.

After we returned to the Captain Cook Hotel I tried to give the trainee an extra pair of Polaroids I'd brought. He seemed shocked and at first refused to accept them. "Then what will you use?" he asked. I pointed out I was still wearing the Polaroids I'd worn the whole time. Satisfied at last, he accepted the glasses like he'd just won the lottery.

Then I fetched an extra pair of flats boots I had, planning also to give them to the trainee so he'd no longer have to leave a bloody trail across the flats. But Mike, as the senior guide, glommed onto them first. He'd been wearing an old, tattered pair of boots that were nearly falling apart, so his feet had hardly any more protection than the trainee's. They also were about three times as wide as my feet, a result of Mike also having spent a lifetime going barefoot, and I didn't see how he could possibly get those huge feet into those flats boots. He seemed to think he could, however—or maybe he planned to sell them and use the money to buy a pair of boots that would fit, if they make them that large. Either way, I hope he was able to make good use of them.

With only one good eye and a trashed back, I regretfully figured I wouldn't be needing those Polaroids or flats boots in the future. I trust I left them in good hands—and feet.

YOU CAN'T EVER HAVE TOO
MANY FLY RODS

IN THE corner of my office is a jumble of metal and plastic tubes that looks like the wreckage of a pipe organ. It's actually my arsenal of fly rods, all kept in tubes to protect them from grandchildren speeding through the house on tricycles. There were thirty-seven rods last time I counted, including seven of cane, twelve of fiberglass, and eighteen of graphite. Some I built myself, others I purchased, and a few were gifts. Several more were won in fly-fishing-club raffles. One was inherited.

Thirty-seven rods might seem like way too many for one fisherman—after all, if you're casting a fly, it's an inescapable fact that you can use only one rod at a time—but I've heard it said, and firmly believe, that an angler can't ever have too many fly rods.

Why? Well, for one thing, I suppose there's pride of ownership, and that applies to at least several of my rods. A few also have historic value, which is reason enough for keeping them. A few others have sentimental attachment.

None of those include rods I built. I've kept them not because they are works of art but for the opposite reason: They were made in a hurry and, with one exception, the workmanship was so sloppy I'm ashamed to have anyone else see them. A couple are graphite, the others fiberglass. Most were built in the late 1960s or early '70s. When I look at them now, which I do rarely, I'm astonished at the thickness of those fiberglass shafts and the stiffness of the cheap metal ferrules I used to join them together. I'm equally amazed at the thickness of the varnish I slathered on them in a futile effort to hide the gaps I left in the windings (it's hard to achieve perfection when your only method for keeping tension on the rod-winding thread is to run it through the pages of a dictionary or a telephone book, with several volumes of an encyclopedia piled on top).

Some of my rods are seldom if ever used. One is the old Goodwin Granger three-piece, nine-foot cane rod I inherited from my father. As a young angler, I used it often before fiberglass rods came along. By then the Granger was showing the signs of many years of hard use, so I decided to refinish it. At the time I had no experience building or refinishing rods, but it looked like a simple enough job.

It wasn't. I soon found I had no idea what to do, or how to do it, so I put the rod away with the intent of resuming work after I'd acquired some experience and skill. Somehow, I've never gotten back to it, and the rod still stands forlornly in its tube, showing the ugly evidence of a would-be craftsman who didn't know his craft. I could have it refinished professionally, but Grangers are not classic rods. So many of them were made that they now have relatively little market value and it would likely cost more than the rod is worth to have it refinished. I may yet do it anyway, just for sentimental reasons; the rod surely deserves better than I have given it.

Another rod I've never used, and would never even think of using, is extremely rare, a Stimson-Lambuth two-piece, nine-foot, spiral-built bamboo rod. It was the fifth such rod built by my late friend and mentor, Letcher Lambuth.

Letcher was one of probably only two rodmakers ever to build spiral rods. He devised his own formula, which called for the rod to be "twisted" one-sixth of a turn between each guide, with six guides—

or one full turn—for each rod section. To achieve this, he mounted door locks on a long, heavy plank, then positioned each freshly glued rod section on the plank, twisted according to his formula, and locked it in place so the twist would remain after the glue set. He used casein glue, the only type then available, reinforcing it with narrow thread windings spaced an inch apart over the full length of the rod. His theory was that the spiral shape of the rod increased the surface area of the bamboo's power fibers, giving the rod more power than a conventional six-sided bamboo rod glued up straight.

The result, at least in the rod I have, is a strong, even, fluid action unlike that of any other bamboo rod I've ever seen. But the rod was more than forty years old when I received it as a gift from Letcher's widow, and given the nature of the old glue holding it together, I have never dared put a line on it. I've only flexed it to test its action, and haven't even done that very many times.

Diabetes robbed Letcher of his sight in the early 1940s, putting an end to his rod-building days, but during the 1960s and early '70s I spent many pleasant hours in his basement workshop where the rafters were still stuffed with culms of Tonkin cane that would have become fly rods if he had still been able to make them. We both knew I wasn't cut out to be a bamboo craftsman, but I still learned a great deal from him about the rodmaker's art, as well as his philosophy that a truly complete angler is one who makes all his own tackle, including flies, lines, nets, creels, fishing vest, and everything else.

The name "Stimson" that appears with Letcher's name on all his rods was to honor his friend Harold Stimson, who made the steel planing form Letcher used to shape his bamboo splines. After Letcher passed away, our mutual friend Al Severeid and I sent the planing form, the plank with the locking mechanisms, one of Letcher's spiral rods, and other paraphernalia to the American Museum of Fly Fishing in Vermont, where they are now part of the museum's collection.

His rod No. 5, now at home in its tube in my office corner, also belongs in a fly-fishing museum, and for years I've hoped we might finally have one in the Pacific Northwest to which I could donate it. We still don't, but I remain hopeful. Meanwhile, the rod remains unfished and undisplayed, but certainly not unappreciated.

Another rod in my collection is an eight-foot, two-section cane rod built by the R. L. Winston Co. The rod, made for a 7-weight line, was well used when I bought it from Walt Johnson, the legendary steel-head fly fisher, who had used it to land several hundred steelhead. Possibly that was why the rod had a "set" in its tip section when I bought it, a slight bend like an arthritic finger. I had the tip section straightened by a professional rod builder in British Columbia, then had the whole thing refinished by Doug Merrick at Winston's old headquarters in San Francisco. When Merrick returned the rod, the words "Built for Steve Raymond" were inscribed on the butt section, erasing the original inscription to Walt Johnson. I had planned to fish the rod, but it looked so pristine and perfect in its refinished condition that I've never had the heart to use it in action. It still looks pristine and perfect in its tube, another candidate for a museum.

Fly fishing has always been peculiarly susceptible to trends, and in the early 1970s the hot trend was to small rods. Lee Wulff was getting lots of publicity using six-foot "midge" rods to land big Atlantic salmon, and Arnold Gingrich praised them lavishly in one of his books. That was enough for me; I had to have one, too, so I built a two-piece, six-foot fiberglass rod for a 6-weight line. That's a heavy line for such a light rod, but I had steelhead in mind. The rod even had a skeleton cork reel seat to save weight. The two sections were joined with a metal ferrule, but after I somehow managed to break the rod's tip section, I replaced it with a new tip and a ferrule made of fiberglass, which saved weight and gave the rod a smoother action. It also enhanced its appearance, and it's the only decent-looking rod I ever made. It was the seventh one I built, so I gave it the serial number 007, optimistically choosing a three-digit numbering system because I thought I might end up building more than a hundred rods in my lifetime. As things eventually turned out, I hardly needed two digits.

I put No. 007 to work trying to emulate Lee Wulff's success by catching a steelhead. I discovered it was easy to hook them on the little rod, but not so easy to land them. My fishing diary relates several unsuccessful hook-ups, including one fish I fought for a long time until it finally headed for a tangled network of snags on the river bottom and I snubbed it hard—too hard—and the leader parted. "I should have landed the fish, and have only my own ineptitude to blame for losing it," my diary says.

I hooked another one soon after. I was in open water with plenty of room and I thought I had a good chance of landing it until the fish started a long run and the hook pulled out. Later, in the same spot, I hooked another. It jumped once before I got it on the reel, then made several short runs and eventually settled down to slug it out at close range. Finally it was exhausted and I landed it, a fine, bright, six-pound female that I released. My quest to take a steelhead on a midge rod was complete.

But the experience left me thinking that landing a big fish on such a small rod was more of a stunt than a legitimate angling feat, and in some ways it wasn't fair to the steelhead; the small rod made it necessary to play the fish much longer than would otherwise have been the case, possibly endangering its survival. So after that I began using the midge rod for fish more suited to its size, mostly trout.

One angry trout almost took the little rod away from me. I was fishing a lake in eastern Washington and had left my fly trailing in the water as I moved from one place to another—never a good idea. A trout suddenly smashed the fly and pulled the rod over the boat's transom before I could react. No.007 disappeared under the surface, along with the precious Hardy reel attached to it, and for a horrible moment I thought both were gone for good. Then I saw a few inches of the rod's tip section pop above the surface and begin moving rapidly across the lake like the periscope of a submarine. It was obvious that air had gotten trapped in the rod's hollow tip section, keeping it above the surface. I started rowing in pursuit as fast as I could. The trout ran a long way with the rod in tow, but the tip section was still above water when the run finally ended. I caught up to it, grabbed the tip, pulled the rod and reel out of the lake, and started reeling in line. To my great surprise the trout was still on and at length I landed and released it, turning what had momentarily seemed a tragedy into a satisfying triumph. Rod No. 007 went on to become one of my all-time favorites. Even in this age of graphite and other exotic composites, I still use it now and then.

In 1969 the Fenwick rod company asked me to ghost-write a casting book for Jim Green, their rod designer and a world-champion caster. My good friend Alan Pratt, chief cartoonist of the *Seattle Times,* was contracted to illustrate the book. Al and I went to West Yellowstone, Montana, to fish with Jim, observe his casting technique, and pick his brain. Lefty Kreh was there, too, and we also fished with him and observed his casting style, very different from Jim's but just as effective in its own way.

Also joining us was Hu Riley, a manufacturer's representative for Fenwick. It was my first meeting with Hu and I was instantly taken with his friendly manner and sense of humor. He lived on Mercer Island in Lake Washington, just east of Seattle, my home at the time, and we became good friends in years to come. Hu also would add several rods to my collection.

Our pleasant "field work" at West Yellowstone eventually led to publication of a vest-pocket-sized paperback titled *Fly Casting from the Beginning,* with Jim's name on the cover as author, although I had done most of the writing. The book led to a continuing relationship with Fenwick, which accounts for the presence of so many Fenwick fiberglass rods in my collection. At that time they were state of the art, and eventually I think I had at least one of every model they made.

One was Fenwick's own effort to capitalize on the midge-rod revolution, a two-section, five-and-a-quarter-foot rod for a 3-weight line,
which is still the smallest rod in my inventory. More about that one
later. Near the opposite end of the Fenwick product line was a model
called the FF80, a two-piece eight-footer designed for a 7-weight line.
It became my favorite weapon for steelhead in rivers and salmon in
salt water, and I fished it so hard I wore one out and had to replace it
with another. In fact, I used the FF80 so often that its timing became
second nature, and it was the first rod I used to cast farther than one
hundred feet.

The middle of Fenwick's lineup included a seven-foot, two-section
model for a 6-weight line, and this became my go-to weapon for dry-
fly fishing in lakes. Like all my other fiberglass rods, it was eventually
superseded by graphite, but I still carry it as a backup.

My introduction to graphite rods came with a phone call. Remem-
bering our earlier collaboration on the little casting book, Jim Green
called and invited Alan Pratt and me to visit Fenwick's rod factory
on Bainbridge Island in Puget Sound and try casting some of the first
graphite rods the company made. He knew our casting styles and
wanted to see how we would fare with the faster actions of the new
high-tech rods.

Al and I took the ferry to Bainbridge on a nasty February morning
and met Jim in a parking lot full of flooded potholes so big they might
have been created by artillery shells. He had half a dozen graphite
rods for us to try, but explained their final designs had not been settled and all the rods had guides temporarily attached with tape so they
could be repositioned easily if necessary. Jim also had the equivalent
models of Fenwick's fiberglass rods on hand so we could compare
them with the new graphites.

We stood in the parking lot under mixed rain and snow and began
casting while Jim watched, listened to our comments, and asked questions. If we said a graphite rod seemed top heavy or unbalanced, or

offered some other criticism, he would sometimes take the rod inside the adjoining shop and reposition the guides, or perhaps even shave a little off the tip, then bring it back and ask us to try it again.

When it was my turn to test the graphite equivalent of the fiberglass FF80, I made several casts of decent length but didn't see or feel anything extraordinary about the new rod. Then I picked up the FF80 for comparison and immediately started throwing much longer casts.

Jim was startled. "You're not supposed to be able to do that!" he said. He asked me to explain how I could cast farther with a fiberglass rod of measurably weaker strength than the new graphite. The only thing I could think of was that I wasn't accustomed to the timing of the new rod but was so familiar with the FF80 that it probably wasn't surprising I could cast farther with it. Jim seemed skeptical, but neither of us could think of another explanation.

After a couple of hours of casting we were all soaked from the rain and snow that kept falling. Jim led us inside where it was warm and dry and, as a reward for our efforts, invited each of us to select a graphite rod blank. I chose a seven-and-a-half-foot, two-section blank Jim said was designed for use with a 6-weight line. He wasn't sure if the butt section was well matched to the tip, though, so he selected a second butt section and suggested I try both to see which worked better.

I mounted reel seats, grips, and guides on both butt sections and tried them. One didn't work at all; it was far too stiff to match up with the more flexible tip section. But the other one matched perfectly, and I had a new seven-and-a-half-foot graphite rod, one of the first ever made. I was so anxious to try it that I wrapped the guides with the only rod-winding thread I had on hand, a miserable urine-yellow color, which eventually led me to nickname the rod "Old Yeller."

I used that rod so hard and so often, in both fresh and salt water (for sea-run cutthroat), that I wore out one full set of guides and had to replace them. I still use it from time to time, although in consideration of its age—now more than forty-five years—I give it plenty of time off. Its full story is told in another book.

By now you probably have the impression that I prefer short rods and 6-weight lines. That's a result of experience. For years I've advanced the theory that stillwater fly fishers would be far better off using short, 5- or 6-weight rods for dry-fly or surface fishing. The reasons should be obvious to anyone who understands the mechanics of casting: Shorter rods have shorter casting strokes and develop higher line speeds, both saving critical time when an angler is trying to deliver a fly quickly to a fast-moving trout. Casting—especially with a double haul—and playing fish also are a lot more fun with such rods. And a 6-weight is heavy enough to deal with all but the strongest wind.

But it's obvious nobody has been listening to my theory. It's now almost impossible to find a commercially made 6-weight rod shorter than nine feet. Did somebody pass a law requiring that all 6-weight rods have to be nine feet long?

One current catalog tells the story, offering listings from six rod manufacturers, including fifty-three different models made for 6-weight lines. Fifty-two of those are nine feet or longer. Only one is less than nine feet—and it's eight and a half feet. There are no smaller 6-weights. You can look in other catalogs and find the same thing.

Just how many nine-foot, 6-weight fly rods does the world need, anyway?

One reason for the apparent popularity of longer 6-weight rods is that many stillwater anglers now fish from float tubes or pontoon boats and must use long rods to keep their backcasts from hitting the water. In my view, anglers who fish from such contrivances handicap themselves unnecessarily, not only because they can't use shorter rods, but also because of their inability to stand up and see what's really going on in the water around them. As a result, they not only penalize their angling effectiveness, but also miss at least half the pleasures and satisfactions of stillwater fly fishing.

Meanwhile, apparently as a minority of one, I continue searching for ever-smaller rods capable of casting 5- or 6-weight lines. I purchased one six-and-three-quarter-foot graphite made for a 6-weight line many years ago, when rod manufacturers evidently had more imagination than they do now. Another rod of the same length was made for me more recently by Don Green when he was president of Sage Manufacturing. I'd told Don my theory that shorter rods were more efficient and suggested that if Sage made some, it might find a market for them. His gracious response was to build a blank to my specifications. It's a fine rod that has given me fine service, but I think it's probably the only six-and-three-quarter-foot, 6-weight rod Sage ever made.

One day I happened to mention my frustrating search for smaller rods to Hu Riley. He said he had some demonstration rods in his garage and might be able to find one I would like. Several days later he came by my house with four or five rods and left them for me to try. I took them to the park next door and tried casting them on grass. None was exactly what I was looking for, but one nevertheless caught my eye. It was a two-piece, seven-and-a-half-foot rod for a 5-weight line, a little longer rod than I wanted. It didn't cast well with a 5-weight, but when I tried it with a 6-weight, it cast beautifully. The manufacturer (not Fenwick) obviously had rated it for the wrong line.

When Hu returned to collect the rods, I asked what he wanted for the seven-and-a-half-footer. "How about some of your books?" he asked. He left my house with several rods under one arm and several books under the other.

A year or two later Hu showed me another rod he thought I might like, a late Fenwick "Iron Feather" graphite. A two-section six-footer with a skeleton cork reel seat, designed for a 5-weight line, it was one of the sweetest little fly rods I'd ever seen. I tried it with a 5.5-weight line and from the first cast I knew this was exactly the rod I wanted. Hu's more-than-generous price was $50.

The "Iron Feather" had probably been designed for small trout in small streams, but I had other purposes in mind. I started using it right away, casting dry flies to rising trout on a local lake. The rod had surprising strength and was a joy to cast. When a good trout took the fly, I felt an almost electric sense of connection with it; every one of the trout's movements was instantly telegraphed through the rod until it seemed as if the trout and I were in some sort of dance, each responding to the movements of the other.

I took the rod to Hosmer Lake in Oregon and used it in similar fashion for the lake's landlocked Atlantic salmon. Other anglers watched in amazement as I caught fish on a rod scarcely more than half the length of theirs. I couldn't remember ever having a rod I felt in tune with so completely, or one I liked as much.

Naturally, I broke it. It was on that same trip to Hosmer. I'd over-shot a cast and the fly caught on a tule. It wouldn't pull loose, so I put down the rod and started maneuvering my pram to go unhook the fly, momentarily neglecting what was happening to the line. The line came taut between the rod and the tule and I heard a sudden terrible snap. The tule had proven stronger than the rod's ultra-slender tip, which broke in half.

I was devastated. That I had nothing but my own carelessness to blame made it even worse. That single moment, that awful snap, put a damper on the whole trip.

When I got home I called Hu, confessed what had happened, and asked if maybe, just maybe, he might have another "Iron Feather" in his inventory. He didn't think so, but said he'd look and let me know.

"You're in luck," he said when he called back. "I do have another one. The rod tube has a dent in it, but the rod itself is fine. It's yours if you want it."

I was willing to pay almost anything, but asked his price as if it were a matter of concern. "Well," Hu said, "why don't we just call this one a gift?" When I protested, he just said, "that's the way I want to do it."

Hu still lived on Mercer Island but by that time I had moved to Whidbey Island in northern Puget Sound, so we had to figure out how to get the rod from Hu's hands into mine. It turned out his daughter also lived on Whidbey, so Hu said he'd give her the rod and I could pick it up at her home, and that's what I did. The new rod was exactly the same as the one I'd broken, and I feel the same deep attachment for it.

Since we now lived far apart, on two different islands, Hu and I didn't have many opportunities to see one another after that, so I was just as surprised as Hu's many other friends the day his face suddenly appeared on television broadcasts and newspaper front pages all over the country.

The story was that historians had finally identified Private First Class Huston Riley of the US Army's First Infantry Division as the wounded GI at Omaha Beach in one of the most famous photographs of World War II. The photo, by famed photographer Robert Capa, was taken as the first wave of troops splashed ashore on the morning of June 6, 1944, and appeared two weeks later on the cover of *Life* magazine. It has since been listed as one of the most important photographic images of the twentieth century.

Several soldiers came forward after the war suggesting they were the GI in the photo, but none could verify his claim. For many years, historians puzzled over the matter, researching service records and other archives in an effort to figure out the soldier's identity. At last they found evidence it was my soft-spoken, amiable, generous friend Hu Riley. The distinctive profile of the soldier in the photo left no doubt of the identification.

Hu had been aboard a landing craft that struck a sandbar about one hundred yards from the beach, forcing him into the water. He stepped off the sandbar into water over his head and tried walking on the bottom until he could no longer hold his breath. Then he activated a pair of life preservers that took him to the surface. Under heavy German fire, he made his way slowly toward the beach and was at the edge of the surf when he was struck in the neck by two bullets. Another soldier and the photographer, whose name Hu never knew, helped him ashore, where he managed to make his way across the beach to rendezvous with other troops from his unit.

Hu was evacuated to England for treatment, but returned to action a short time later and saw more heavy fighting. In October 1944, he was severely wounded again, this time near the German city of Aachen. Once more he was evacuated to England, then to the United States, where he was discharged from the Army in September 1945.

All of which I hadn't known—nor, I think, did most of Hu's friends.

After the story broke, Tom Brokaw of NBC News interviewed Hu at his Mercer Island home. The television broadcast showed them standing on the dock in front of Hu's home on Lake Washington, both casting fly rods.

On October 2, 2011, Hu passed away at the age of ninety. I miss him and think of him often, especially when I'm using my replacement "Iron Feather." He was a true American hero and a great friend. I'm proud and privileged to have known him.

My collection of rods recently expanded to thirty-eight, again because I got lucky in a raffle. This time it was a nine-foot, four-piece graphite rod for a 5-weight line. I found a cloth bag that fit it and a rod tube of the right size and put it away along with the other "pipe organ" remains in my office corner. Maybe one day I'll donate it to a worthy cause and someone else can win it. Or maybe it will make a good rod for one of my lively granddaughters.

As I said, you can't ever have too many fly rods. Still, I think maybe it's about time I stopped buying raffle tickets.

SINGLE ACTION

EACH YEAR fly-fishing catalogs display a flashy array of new reels. Some cost more than the first car I drove, but that's mostly a reflection of my increasing age and the declining value of the dollar. I hope I'm in better shape than the dollar.

These glittering new reels are light years ahead of those I used as a young fisherman. Most were hand-me-downs from my father or one of my uncles, but they served me well until I started earning enough money to buy something more sophisticated (newspaper reporters traditionally aren't paid very well). I hardly ever throw anything away, though, and now several of those old reels are on display in my office.

Most of my office shelves are crammed with books, but two are reserved for the clutter of my fly-fishing life—photos of old fishing partners, most now long departed, a couple of fly plates, a painting or two, some Canadian fly-pattern postage stamps, old fly boxes, other bric-a-brac, and the small collection of reels. In addition to the old hand-me-downs there are several newer reels, consigned to the shelf because they were tried and found wanting in some respect.

One of the old hand-me-downs is the centerpiece of a shadowbox display crafted by my friend Gil Nyerges, the most prolific fly tyer

I've ever known and an artist at framing things. The reel is an old Pflueger Gem that belonged to my father, though I also used it a few years. It was probably made in the mid-1930s and I liked it because it had a loud click, which most of my other inherited reels lacked. I like loud clicks.

The reel shares the shadowbox with a photo of my father landing a trout in British Columbia's Hi Hium Lake, sometime around 1940. An array of his old flies, artfully arranged by Gil, surrounds the photo and the reel. The display was Gil's idea, and when I tried to pay for it he told me to buy him dinner instead and we'd call it even. I hope he enjoyed the dinner as much as I enjoy seeing his fine work every day, but I doubt it.

The other reels in my little collection are poised on another shelf. All are single-action reels, the only type I've ever owned or used (yeah, I know; these days "single action" sounds like an internet dating website). I've never seen a useful purpose for multiplying reels, and anyway, they seem too complicated for a simple guy like me. As for "automatic" reels, I don't think any self-respecting fly fisher would ever be found with one in his or her possession.

The reel occupying the front spot on one side of the shelf is an old Ocean City Model 306, known as the "Wanita." The origins of this reel date to the 1920s, but it went through so many small changes in its long history that it's now nearly impossible to tell exactly when an individual reel was manufactured, although the one on my shelf was probably made before World War II. It earned the front spot on my shelf through hard service in a role its designers probably never intended for it.

After I inherited it, the reel remained unused for several years until I began fishing for sea-run cutthroat in Puget Sound. Since that meant I'd be fishing in salt water, I wanted a reel that would resist corrosion and wouldn't be a great loss if it didn't. That's why I choose the Ocean City; with a name like that, you'd think it was made for saltwater use.

Maybe it was. It's ruggedly built, three and a half inches in diameter with a black finish, and both front and back plates are closed, without holes for ventilation. The only moving part is the spool, another reason I thought it would be a good saltwater reel—there was hardly anything that could go wrong with it. It also has the very simplest (and probably most reliable) form of check—a short, heavy spring around the base of the hollow spindle on which the pool rotates. A small screw holds the crank plate to the spindle, and when the screw is tightened it forces the inside edge of the spool against the spring, which then keeps the spool under tension so it can't turn freely in either direction. That keeps the reel from overrunning when line is being pulled on or off by an angler or a fish (a check is not the same as a drag system, which is usually adjustable and designed to increase tension on the line when a fish is running; the Ocean City had no drag).

The average sea-run cutthroat isn't very large—three pounds would be exceptional—and although they're hard fighters, they typically don't run very far, so the Ocean City seemed a good match. I loaded it with backing and a weight-forward monofilament intermediate sinking line, which I've always liked for fishing sea-runs because you can easily control the depth you're fishing; if you want the fly to go deeper, you just wait a little while until it sinks farther.

The reel worked perfectly for my intended purpose. Corrosion didn't seem to be an issue and several times I hooked cutthroat large or strong enough to pull a few turns of line off the reel, but it never overran and the check never applied enough tension to pop the leader. I even landed a few small salmon on it. I fished it several years and never had a single backlash or any other problem.

I didn't know a much bigger test was coming.

It happened on a cold, clear January afternoon. I'd been fishing for hours on an outgoing tide with only a single cutthroat to show for my efforts. Now the tide was swiftly emptying the small estuary I was

fishing, apparently trying to see if it could drain the estuary before
the sun sank below the row of ragged fir trees along the shore. Things
had been quiet a long time and I was about to give up hope when a
sizable fish broke water not far away. I cast to the spot and started
retrieving, but nothing happened; whatever fish had made the rise
apparently wasn't interested in my fly. It had looked like a big fish,
though, so I clipped off the small fly I'd been using, replaced it with
a larger pattern, and cast again to the spot.

This time the fly was taken hard by a strong fish that started a
long run across the shallow flats of the rapidly emptying estuary. The
Ocean City spit line in eerie silence as it tried to keep up with the fish,
which finally revealed itself in a magnificent leap—a chrome-bright
steelhead whose sides flashed brilliantly in the fading light. But when
it returned to the water, my fly was no longer in its mouth.

I tried a few more casts, but the tide was now running so fast I
knew I'd have to hurry back or my small boat and I would end up
on an isolated sandbar for half the cold night until the tide returned.
Reluctantly, I pulled anchor and started rowing hard against the rushing outflow of water. It was tough going, but eventually I reached a
large tidal pool not far from where my truck was parked on the shore.
I was pretty well worn out from battling the tide, so I stopped to rest
for a moment in the quiet water. Automatically, I surveyed the pool,
which was about a hundred yards in diameter. Oysters were beginning to show their craggy shells above the sinking tide around the
edges of the pool.

Then I saw something else—a small, subtle rise. Probably a cutthroat, I thought. I'd pulled in my line long before, but it was still
lying in loose coils on the boat deck, so I picked up my rod, false
cast to work out line, delivered the fly to the vicinity of the rise, and
began a quick retrieve. A rising mound of water appeared behind the
fly and followed in fast pursuit, then abruptly turned away and disappeared. Based on its size, I knew the pursuing fish was probably
another steelhead. As if in confirmation, a large, gleaming shape cut

through the surface nearby, and even before the ripples from that rise had disappeared I saw several more rises. It looked as if at least a dozen steelhead were in the pool, waiting for the tide to return and lift them closer to their destination, a small stream at the head of the estuary.

In the next hour, until it was too dark to see and almost too shallow to float my boat, I hooked five steelhead. One slipped the hook immediately after the strike, another ran into the oysters and broke off, but I landed and released the others. All were fresh-run fish, superbly bright and in peak condition, and fought with twice the strength of a river-hooked steelhead. The largest was twelve pounds and the smallest about half that size. They made the spool of the poor old Ocean City spin in a blur, forcing it to yield line and backing as never before, then gain it back while I cranked the spool as never before. I doubt the people who designed and built that reel ever dreamed it would be put to such a test. I hadn't either, but the old reel proved quietly and unspectacularly equal to the task.

After that I tested the Ocean City against steelhead on several more occasions, most notably a great day when I hooked eight and landed six. The two escapees were my fault, not the reel's. I always carefully released every steelhead I caught in salt water because they were wild, native fish, belonging to small, vulnerable runs.

I fished that reel several more seasons and it never failed. But one day I was signing books at a fly-fishing show and got to talking with a reel manufacturer who was displaying his latest wares. He offered to trade one of his new reels for a signed copy of one of my books, and although I didn't really think I needed a new reel, it seemed too good an offer to refuse. So we made the swap.

The new reel was a handsome thing, carefully machined from aluminum bar stock and anodized within an inch of its life to prevent corrosion. It also had a high-tech, adjustable drag system, with settings that seemed to range from "help yourself" to "hold everything." The reel's only fault was that it, like the Ocean City, was silent, or nearly so, although if you listened very closely (and perhaps used a stethoscope) you could hear a very soft click when you reeled in.

After pondering what to do with the new reel, I decided its extra-strength anodizing would make it good for saltwater use. It lacked sufficient line capacity for large quarry, however, so by default it became the replacement for the Ocean City. After more than sixty years of faithful service to my father and me, I figured the old reel had earned a graceful retirement berth on my cluttered shelf, where it's been ever since.

Even before I retired the Ocean City, I had noticed to my infinite regret that the precious small runs of wild steelhead that once returned to the diminutive estuaries of Puget Sound had all but vanished, victims of the cumulative effects of logging, "development," and other environmental abuses. That meant I never had a chance to test the new reel against a fresh-run saltwater steelhead. But one banner day when I was prospecting for cutthroat, I blundered into a posse of bright, feisty coho salmon and exercised nine of them on the new reel. It performed well, if in almost total silence, but a six-pound coho is not the same as a twelve-pound saltwater steelhead, so the reel got off easy. I still use it, though it's never earned the same respect I had for the old Ocean City.

I have to admit the new reel is prettier, though.

The front position on the other side of the shelf is occupied by a Hardy Featherweight reel. It's in near-mint condition, so people ask me what it's doing there with a bunch of old reels. It was one of several Hardy reels I bought back in the 1970s, when you could still get them for less than a week's pay. Their great and well-earned reputation for reliability was one reason I got them; another was that I've always liked Hardys for the lovely racket they make when a big fish is taking line. The Featherweight is the only one I no longer use, not because anything is wrong with it but because it turned out to be too small for my intended purpose. That was my fault, not the reel's.

I was at the height of my obsession with small rods when I bought
the reel. I had acquired the previously mentioned five-and-a-quarter-
foot Fenwick rod for a 3-weight line, and thought the Featherweight
would make a perfect companion. Then I discovered that even a
double-tapered 3-weight line would barely fit on the Featherweight's
diminutive spool, leaving no room at all for backing. At first that
didn't overly concern me because I planned to use the little rod for
little fish—trout of twelve or fourteen inches or less. It worked fine
for that purpose—I never had a fish take more than a few turns of line
off the reel—and when the big Atlantic salmon began to disappear
from Oregon's Hosmer Lake in the early 1980s, I thought the little
rod and reel would be a good match for the much smaller landlocked
Atlantics being stocked to replace them.

For years, Hosmer had been one of my favorite places. It was
stocked originally with hatchery-reared descendants of sea-run Atlantic salmon from Quebec. They adapted quickly to the lake's heavy
caddis and mayfly hatches and many reached weights of four to six
pounds, sometimes more. For more than a decade Hosmer provided
some of the best dry-fly fishing anywhere.

But the sea-run stock had always been difficult to handle in the
hatchery, with less than desirable survival rates. Continual interbreed-
ing also led to increasing genetic defects—loose scales and short gill
covers being most evident. Biologists who managed the lake said the
sea-run fish also had a bad habit of escaping over the lake's outlet
dam at high water, after which they disappeared into watery caverns,
never to be seen again. No matter how many salmon were stocked,
fish numbers in the lake continued to decline, and when it finally
became obvious the hatchery program just wasn't working anymore,
the state went looking for new fish. It settled on landlocked Atlantics
from Lake Sebago, Maine.

The landlocks were very different fish. They were accustomed to
feeding on forage fish in their native habitat and never did fully adapt
to Hosmer's prolific insect hatches, nor did they rise as freely as the

old sea-run fish. They also ranged deeper, keeping their noses in the muck so persistently that they actually carved trenches in the lake's shallow bottom. Worst of all, they didn't live as long or grow nearly as large as the sea-runs. Salmon of more than twenty inches became rare; most seemed to top out around fourteen or fifteen inches.

That's what made me think it was time to start using my little rod and the Hardy Featherweight. But just to make sure, I fished several days without seeing a single big fish before deciding to risk the little rod and the reel without any backing. You can guess what happened: When I stood to make my initial cast with the little outfit, the first salmon I saw was the largest I'd seen during the entire trip. There was no time to pick up another rod, so I cast ahead of the cruising salmon and watched it rise obediently and suck in the fly.

The ensuing fight would have been a real nail-biter if I'd had the luxury of biting my nails while it was underway. The little Hardy sang its electrifying song as the salmon ran until the spool's bare metal was showing through the last few turns of line, and I waited for the inevitable outcome—a broken leader or, worse, a lost line. But the salmon blessedly stopped short just as it looked as if it would strip the spool, giving me a chance to regain line. Then we went through the whole business again, several times, until the salmon finally tired and I brought it to hand. It measured twenty-five inches and I guessed its weight around five pounds—the biggest fish of the trip, and certainly one of the very last big fish in Hosmer.

That was the Hardy Featherweight's single moment of glory. After that experience, I decided I didn't want to run the risk of getting "spooled" again, so I retired the reel. It now occupies the front spot on my shelf by virtue of being so small it would disappear if I put another reel ahead of it.

Behind the Featherweight, and looming over it, is a battered Beaudex reel, one of five models made by the old British firm of J. W. Young & Sons. I won it in a raffle back in the 1960s and thought it was my lucky day; it was the first addition to what was then my meager assortment of hand-me-down reels. It also was the first reel I'd had that seemed large and rugged enough for steelhead or salmon. Not only that, it also had an adjustable drag and a reasonably loud click. What more could anyone ask? At length I discovered one could have asked for quite a lot more, because the Beaudex turned out to have several critical faults.

I started fishing the reel for Kamloops trout in British Columbia, and while the great majority of those fish don't reach salmon or steelhead size, they are far and away the hardest-fighting trout I've ever encountered. The Beaudex held its own against them, which I thought proved it capable of bigger things. Unfortunately, I badly overestimated how much bigger.

I found out one day when I went fishing for fresh-run Chinook salmon in the lower tidal reaches of a large river. The tide was flooding and the salmon were hard on its heels. I could see them rolling nearly everywhere in the large expanse of water, fish ranging from ten to maybe thirty pounds—larger fish than I had ever caught. I started fishing a large fly, which I thought appropriate for fish of such size, but the salmon ignored it, so I replaced it with a smaller pattern and hooked a fish immediately. It exploded out of the water in a great flash of silver and popped the leader as if it were a cobweb. Nervously, I tied on a heavier leader and resumed fishing. I hooked four more salmon on the small fly, but the hook pulled out of each one and none was on long enough to give the Beaudex a workout.

Frustrated, I replaced the fly with a larger one, but the salmon ignored it as before, so I finally switched back to the small pattern. A big salmon took the fly near the end of my first retrieve and ran with awesome power. The Beaudex began yielding line with a baritone stutter that rose in frequency to a near falsetto; music to my ears! But I barely had a chance to appreciate it before the reel seized up, the leader snapped, and the fish disappeared—all in less time than it takes to tell it. I'd found the limits of the Beaudex's capabilities.

After the reel cooled off, I doused its innards with oil and grease until it resumed functioning and I kept using it even though the salmon episode cost whatever faith the reel had earned from me; it was still the largest-capacity reel I had.

Then I found another fault, which I should have noticed in the beginning: The Beaudex's reel foot was attached to the reel with a pair of small screws; most reels use rivets for that purpose. I discovered that one day when the reel suddenly fell off my rod in mid-cast; the screws had become fatally loose. It took some searching to find replacements of the right size, so when I finally found them I purchased several to carry in my fishing vest with a small screwdriver to make emergency repairs. I also began periodically checking and tightening the screws.

Despite these precautions, disaster eventually caught up to me again. I was playing a summer steelhead in the North Fork of the Stillaguamish when it happened; the fish started a long downstream run and I was heading for the beach to follow when a backlash suddenly formed on the Beaudex and it abruptly stopped turning. I pulled frantically at the snarled coils of line, trying to free it, when the screws let go again and the reel fell into the river. Desperately, I scooped it up and continued downstream in pursuit of the fish. As I did, I found that if I held both the rod and reel in my left hand and kept the reel pressed tight against the rod grip, I could wind the reel with my right hand.

I managed to gain enough line that way to cover up the backlash, and when the fish started another run I chased as fast as I could to keep it from taking the line covering the backlash. The steelhead finally stopped in some quiet water and, after a long, stubborn, and very awkward struggle (at least on my part), I guided it to the beach—a bright hen fish that I measured at twenty-eight inches before release.

By then I thought the Beaudex was probably jinxed. Subsequent events seemed to confirm my suspicions; somehow—maybe it got banged against a rock or something—the reel got out of alignment and would no longer turn in either direction. Lubricants didn't help, and my clumsy application of force succeeded only in breaking off a piece of the spool's ventilated plate.

That was the last straw, and the Beaudex went on the shelf.

The biggest reel in my little collection of has-beens is a Cortland S/S Magnum. I bought it before my first trip to Christmas Island, not because it was a high-end reel—it wasn't—but because the trip was expensive, I was on a budget, and the Cortland was the lowest-priced reel that had the features I wanted. Made in England, it was corrosion-resistant with an adjustable drag and had a relatively noisy click. Most important, it also had capacity for a weight-forward 7-weight line plus 200 yards of backing. You rarely need that much backing for bonefish, but on those occasions when you do need that much, you *really* need it.

The Cortland performed satisfactorily on that trip and I took it along on my first visit to Salmon Brook Camp on the main Southwest Miramichi in New Brunswick several years later. Initially, the reel did its job there, too; on my first day I hooked a large Atlantic salmon and played it almost to the beach before the hook pulled out, and later I landed a nine-pound fish and several grilse. Toward the end of the week, however, I noticed the reel's click was functioning unevenly. When I opened the reel I found that the screw holding one of the pawls in place had come loose. I tightened it as best I could and finished out the week with no further problems.

The reel accompanied me on another trip to Christmas Island a year later. Right away I noticed the click was again starting to run in hit-and-miss fashion—definitely not something you want when fishing for bonefish. I opened the reel and found the same screw loose again, and when I tried tightening it I discovered its threads were stripped. Finding a replacement screw on Christmas Island was out of the question, so I coated the screw with epoxy cement and reset it as best I could. It worked OK for the next day or two.

The end came on the best day of bonefishing I've ever had, before or since. Wading a shallow flat, I hooked fish after fish, and after every release it seemed I'd look up and see another within casting range. Nearly all ran as only bonefish can run, usually well into the backing, but my emergency repair to the Cortland seemed to be holding up.

Until it didn't. I'd hooked another fish, no larger than most of the others, and it was well into its first run when the reel suddenly fell silent, started spinning freely, and big loops of line flew in all directions, forming a giant snarl that caught in the rod's stripping guide, causing the leader to snap. I opened the reel, found the screw broken in half and the once-attached pawl completely missing. Retrieving my line by hand, I stowed it and the broken reel in my fanny pack and took out the backup reel I was carrying.

The backup was an old Hardy St. John. I'd brought it because it had adequate line and backing capacity, but it wasn't made for saltwater use and I knew I'd have to wash it in fresh water and apply lubricants lavishly after each use. I put it on and went right back to catching bonefish, enjoying the day even more because of the Hardy's joyful racket. I used the St. John for the rest of the week, washing, drying, and anointing it with oil after every use. It worked perfectly; it still does, though it hasn't been used in salt water since that trip.

The Cortland, meanwhile, was banished forever to my shelf of old and broken reels.

I keep these reels because they remind me of good times (mostly) on pleasant waters. All are silent now—of course, the Ocean City always was—but sometimes, when I see them sitting there on my cluttered shelf, I think I can still faintly hear the music of the others in my mind.

I hope to keep hearing it until it's my turn to go on the shelf.

INVASIVE SPECIES

His HAIR was iron-gray, his eyes level and penetrating, his face as rugged and craggy as his name, which was Lee Wulff. He was the most famous fly fisherman in the world.

It was a reputation he had not gained by happenstance. Lee had fished almost everywhere, it seemed, and for almost everything, and his adventures had been widely chronicled in magazine articles, books, movies, and television shows. I was in awe of him, as I suppose every other young angler was at the time, so when my wife, Joan, and I were invited to dinner with Lee and his wife, also named Joan, we were only too pleased to accept.

The invitation was from our friends Lew and Elizabeth Bell. Lew was president of what was then known as the Federation of Fly Fishermen. He and I had worked together previously on a couple of conservation projects, but we still didn't know one another well when he asked me to join the organization's board and serve as secretary, and I agreed. As we started trying to get a grip on a young, far-flung organization with virtually no infrastructure, we became close friends, and so did our wives, who turned out to be members of the same sorority.

The dinner would be at Lew and Elizabeth's home and it would be just the six of us.

The gathering was convivial and the conversation varied and interesting, and when dinner was over Lee and I retired to Lew's spacious living room, each with drink in hand, and resumed our conversation in front of the fireplace. Because the subject was on both our minds, it was probably inevitable that we soon began talking about the future of fly fishing—or, more specifically, about public versus private waters.

Lee's experience, mostly in the East, had made him decidedly pessimistic about the future of public fishing. He had witnessed the wholesale decline and destruction of public waters from rapid population growth and urban sprawl in the East until the only remaining decent fishing was in private ownership, and the only way to gain access was to pay for it. He was convinced the same thing eventually would happen in my native Pacific Northwest, and I would live to see the day when our only good fishing also would be private and expensive.

I was about thirty years old then, full of enthusiasm and convinced that fishing was and always would be an egalitarian sport with opportunities for all who lived in the Northwest. After all, we had a lot more water than most of the rest of the country, nearly all of it was open to the public, the resident human population was relatively small, and it was still possible to reach quality fishing within short driving distance, even from a city the size of Seattle. I told Lee I didn't think I would live long enough to see the end of that.

Lee quietly sipped his drink while I argued my case. When I was finished, he smiled a little—or maybe it was a grimace—and said: "You'll see."

Nearly five decades have passed since that conversation, and I now wish to acknowledge that Lee was right and I was wrong.

It happened with breathtaking speed. Seattle, which always had been a somewhat provincial city tucked away in the remote northwest corner of the country, suddenly became everybody's darling destination. It was dubbed the nation's "most livable city," and people flocked from every direction, even from the west across the Pacific. Almost overnight, Seattle became a crowded metropolitan melting pot.

Geographically confined to a narrow hourglass of land between Lake Washington and Elliott Bay on Puget Sound, the city quickly spilled over its boundaries and metastasized in all directions into the countryside. Bellevue, a once quiet little town east of Lake Washington, grew quickly into one of the state's largest cities, a crowded, ugly, unfriendly place built for automobiles instead of people. Tract homes filled the river valleys and crawled up the Cascade foothills, and many little lakes and streams where in past years I'd enjoyed fly fishing for trout began sprouting houses on all sides, as if someone had planted them and added fertilizer.

The Green River, where as a young angler I had good trout fishing among pastoral farms and truck gardens, became an industrial sump, with wall-to-wall warehouses, shopping malls, industries, freeways, and endless traffic. The river is now known mostly for occasionally inundating the homes and businesses built stupidly in its flood plain, and as the dumping spot for victims of the infamous Green River serial killer.

The rising blight also spread far beyond Seattle. Central Oregon and southern British Columbia, where I used to spend much of my fishing time, have both been similarly overrun with people and pollution and I seldom go to either place anymore.

And so it is throughout the West and, I assume, the rest of the country. Almost before we knew what was happening, the beauty, tranquility, and fishing we had enjoyed and long taken for granted was all but gone, taken from us as if by a thief in the night. We had been blindsided by an unstoppable invasive species.

The invasive species was us.

Runaway population growth is now a fact nearly everywhere, responsible for virtually every environmental, economic, and social problem we have. We have met the enemy and he is us—and us, and us, and us. When the epitaph for the human race is written, I'm convinced it will say "They bred to death."

Meanwhile, every day there are more fishermen, fewer fish, and fewer places to fish.

We should have known it was coming, for such things have been going on a long time. For evidence of that we need look no further than the prescient words of the Renaissance poet Thomas Bastard (1566–1616), who, with a name like that, must have had a difficult life. Maybe that's why he took up fishing.

Anyway, this is how he appraised the situation in sixteenth-century England:

> *Fishing, if I a fisher may protest,*
> *Of pleasures is the sweetest, of sports the best,*
> *Of exercises the most excellent.*
> *Of recreations the most innocent.*
> *But now the sport is marred, and wot, ye, why?*
> *Fishes decrease, and fishers multiply.*

Imagine what Bastard would think if he were here today. Fishes are decreasing and fishers increasing more rapidly than ever, and much of the trout and steelhead fishing that once flourished in the Pacific Northwest has been severely degraded or lost altogether. The public fishing that was once widely available and accessible to almost everybody is now a thing of the past. The few good public waters that remain are usually restricted in some way, often to fly-fishing or artificial lures only, and have daily limits of only a single trout or at most a few. It's also no surprise that these waters are overwhelmingly crowded. Widespread illegal planting of largemouth bass and other non-native species has ruined scores of other waters. Now anglers who want to fish in solitude with a reasonable chance of catching large trout in relatively unspoiled surroundings must seek private waters and pay to fish them.

This might be a good time to define exactly what I mean by private waters. The Pacific Northwest always has had some waters that were private, at least in the sense that physical access to them meant paying a fee. But most of these places were fishing camps, and the fee also included overnight accommodations, boats, meals, and other services, all in a package, so customers got a lot more for their money than just access to the water. The camps were open to everybody and, at least in the beginning, the fees were reasonable and affordable for most people. So maybe it was an illusion, but it never seemed as if people were paying just to fish; instead, they were paying for a whole fishing vacation, and the cost just happened to include fishing privileges.

I remember there were still a few of these camps scattered in the hills around Puget Sound when I began fishing seriously as a young man, and I patronized some without a second thought. All have since disappeared, but others remain in nearby British Columbia and I continue to patronize several of those. Nearly all provide everything necessary for a complete fishing vacation, including access to the water, and it still seems as if patrons are getting a lot more for their money than just the privilege of fishing. I've also become friends with many camp owners, and I understand very well how hard they must work to keep such places going, and how tenuous is the modest living they earn from their efforts. So I don't begrudge their fees, even though they have necessarily increased along with the cost of nearly everything else.

What's different now is that we are seeing more and more places where one has to pay *just to fish,* with nothing else thrown in; you might even have to bring your own float tube or boat, and you will have to arrange your own meals and lodging. These places, where all your money buys is a few hours of fishing time, are what I now define as private waters. They are usually lakes, ponds, or stretches of river located on private property, and their cost of operation is only what it takes to stock them annually with trout—which, in the case of rivers, may not even be necessary—or to buy a few pounds of hatchery pellets to supplement what nature provides. So fees paid by fishermen are mostly pure profit for the owners of these places, which often are little more than fish feedlots. Small wonder there are more such waters all the time.

I have an inherent distrust for anyone who tries to make a living from fly fishing, but in the case of the owners of private waters, they usually have at least something invested in the enterprise, so I think they have a legitimate right to charge fishermen, although some charge far more than is reasonable. These waters also are often booked through fly-fishing shops, which may receive a share of the fee, and in some cases such fees are a major source of their income.

A few shops publish printed or online catalogs that include elaborate descriptions of private waters, and these always make interesting reading. At least one shop has gone to some lengths to explain in its catalog *why* private waters have become necessary. Years ago, the catalog says, the shop "recognized that the demand for angling privacy and quality fishing had far outstripped all but the most remote public resources. Then we did something about it . . . We began looking for fishing spots where fly rodders might enjoy quality, secluded fly fishing for a modest fee . . . As advocates for public fishing, we decided right away against exploiting any private waters that were historically open to the public. Most of our current private waters fishing destinations have been posted and off-limits to the public for generations. Some have been behind locks and fences for more than a century. . . .

"All of our Private Waters [capitalization in original] are managed exclusively as catch-and-release destinations, and we allow only fly fishing with barbless hooks. The angling pressure is kept intentionally light in order to ensure each guest enjoys as fine a fly-fishing experience as possible."

It sounds good, but is it just my imagination or is there a hint of defensiveness in all this? Or perhaps a touch of guilt over the notion of making people pay to fish?

In any case, the shop considers $135 a day "a modest fee" if you choose only to fish and not book accommodations. And that *is* a modest fee compared to many other private waters.

This shop's commitment to stay away from waters historically open to the public is also commendable. Others apparently aren't so concerned about the privatization of public waters; they offer private fishing on waters that were once open to anyone with a fishing license, apparently without feeling any guilt about it.

Is all this a good thing or a bad thing? I suppose the answer depends at least partly on your income. Fly fishing has become a much more expensive sport than it used to be, even for those who don't fish private waters. All the equipment costs much more—rods, reels, fly lines, waders, accessories (and now there are many more "essential" accessories than in years past), hooks, vises, fly-tying materials—you name it. A beginning fly fisher must be prepared to make a sizable investment just to get started, especially if he or she also signs up for one of the numerous fly-fishing schools now being offered. And all that before making the first cast.

This has serious implications for the future of fly fishing. The sport has always depended on a relatively steady influx of young anglers, but these days many young people face economic circumstances that make it difficult or impossible to take up the sport. Recent college graduates have student loans that must be paid. Returning veterans must cope with a tough job market and often have to settle for low pay. Young married couples struggle with childcare costs or mortgages. In each case, there's little or nothing left over for fly fishing or almost anything else.

Under these circumstances, if you're going to start fly fishing, you *really* have to want to do it. That could mean buying your equipment at garage sales or thrift stores, then trying to find fishing in hard-pressed public waters close to home—not a good recipe for developing a long-term commitment to the sport.

Not that many young people are now likely to get involved in fly fishing in any event. In my generation, it was typical for parents to expose their children to camping and fly fishing at a very young age, as my parents did with me, so that by the time I was old enough to make my own decisions, fly fishing was at the top of my priority list. Many of my contemporaries had similar introductions to the sport. Unfortunately, that's not the case anymore. These days, families that take their kids camping or fishing seem the exception rather than the rule. Instead of becoming acquainted with the inspirations and attractions of an outdoor life, most kids now sit indoors watching videos, playing videogames, texting, or tweeting. By the time they have their own disposable incomes, they're thinking only of buying the next electronic toy instead of a new fly rod.

Some people might think this is good. After all, if there are fewer up-and-coming fly fishers, that will leave more room on public waters for the rest of us.

But that in turn raises hard questions for the future of the sport. Fewer fly fishers also will necessarily mean less support for preservation or restoration of the threatened public resources on which we still depend—rivers, lakes, salt waters, and the fish that inhabit them. The absence of a large public constituency to speak in defense of these things will simply make it easier for "developers" to have their way, which will mean even fewer quality fishing waters in the future. That will surely lead to increasing demand for expensive private waters in a self-perpetuating cycle that could consign future fly fishers to a small minority of well-heeled anglers who can afford such fisheries and the expensive equipment needed to fish them. Fly fishing will then truly become the elite "doctors' and lawyers' sport" it has always been wrongly accused of being.

Other than well-heeled, what kind of anglers will these people be? It's easy to imagine a scenario where most future fly fishers will get out fishing only a week or two each year—the pressures of making money occupying nearly all the rest of their time—and those few trips will be to expensive private waters where anglers will usually fish under the close supervision of professional guides who tell them where, when, and how to fish and what fly to use. In other words, these future so-called fly fishers will rarely if ever have to learn the intricacies of the sport, study its literature, or think for themselves; instead, they'll always have a well-paid guide to tell them what to do.

What will that mean for the future of the sport? Or its literature and traditions? The implications are obvious.

That's a pretty bleak outlook for the future, but it's not just a figment of my imagination. I've heard the same thoughts expressed around numerous campfires shared with other anglers, most of them nearly as old as I am. Some of those same thoughts also emerged in my long-ago conversation with Lee Wulff.

What can we do about all this? The answer seems to be: not much. It's a bigger problem than any individual or any group can hope to solve. It will take social and economic upheavals of enormous magnitude to change the circumstances that have brought us to this point, a fundamental shift in public attitudes that will make people turn off their phones and TVs and rediscover the outdoors, a monumental change in economic conditions that will give more people the wherewithal to enjoy fly fishing, and a huge societal shift for people to start having smaller families.

The odds against that happening seem astronomical. Meanwhile, it would be a fine thing if some of the owners of private waters would donate occasional free days to fly-fishing clubs or other conservation groups that could raffle them off for fund-raising purposes. This would give fishermen who otherwise can't afford private waters at least a chance to fish a few of them, while simultaneously supporting worthy causes. It also would probably do a lot to enhance the reputations of the owners.

It might be good for their souls as well.

My income is above the poverty line but not enough to allow many trips to private waters. I have fished a few, though, and sometimes the fishing lived up to advance billing and sometimes it didn't. But uncertainty always plays a part in fishing, and even on expensive private lakes or streams you can't escape nasty weather. So far I've not heard of anyone offering refunds for a bad day due to weather, lack of a good hatch, or other adverse circumstances.

I wish I had a refund for the day I spent on the most expensive private water I ever fished. When I got up early that morning, the radio reported the local temperature was twenty-six degrees. That's Fahrenheit, not centigrade. It hadn't warmed more than a couple of degrees by the time we reached the lake we had paid to fish. I'd heard fabulous tales of its big fighting rainbow and I was looking forward to exercising some of those leviathans, but the lake looked about as inviting as a new ice age. Patches of thin ice hugged the shoreline and the rest of the lake looked like it also might freeze at any moment.

There was no sign of rising fish, which made me think the trout were probably smarter than the four of us who had come to fish for them; the trout at least had sense enough not to thrust their noses into the cold air, which was more than we could say. Even the sagebrush on the surrounding hillsides looked brittle and frozen. But we had paid dearly for the privilege of fishing, so there was nothing left to do but try it. Mercifully, by the time we got on the water the temperature had warmed enough so that we could cast without clots of ice forming in the rod guides, although that was about the weather's only concession.

I quickly noted my three companions were all chironomid fishermen. That can be either a positive or a pejorative term, depending on your viewpoint. The usual chironomid fishing technique involves determining the depth, either by physical measurement or use of an electronic device, then tying on a leader of sufficient length to reach within a foot or so of the bottom. A weighted chironomid pupa imitation is attached to the end of the leader tippet and a floating strike indicator is fixed to the leader butt, which is attached to a floating fly line. The angler casts the whole affair as far as it is possible to cast such a rig, sits back to wait while the fly sinks, then hunkers down to stare at the strike indicator, waiting for it to dip suddenly beneath the surface—the signal that a trout has taken the suspended imitation.

In the hands of someone who knows what he's doing, this can be a deadly method, and it was evident my friends knew what they were doing; they were all soon playing fish. But that method of fishing never has been my cup of tea; I enjoy casting, especially to rising fish, and I like to keep moving, trying to take fish in different places or by different means. In other words, I like the exercise involved in fly fishing, and the sight of motionless, hunched-over chironomid fishermen seems the antithesis of that. They look frozen even when it's warm. Not much exercise in that.

But to each his own. I fished in my usual way, first prospecting unsuccessfully for rising fish, then trying various fly patterns in various places, using different retrieves and fishing at different depths in hopes of finding a combination appealing to the trout. I never had a touch, while my comrades continued hooking fish steadily.

The morning passed coldly and our foursome went ashore to eat lunch. We gathered at a picnic table—an amenity thrown in by the management at no extra charge—but when we sat down I noticed all my friends were careful to keep their distance from me. I understood why; they had been watching me, knew I hadn't hooked a fish all morning, and feared whatever ill luck I was suffering might be contagious if they got too close.

Afternoon was a repeat of morning. My companions kept catching fish on chironomid imitations and I continued catching nothing. After a couple more hours of this, I began to hear the meter running in my head; I had paid a hefty sum to fish this lake, time was running out, and my investment was running out with it.

Maybe that's a hidden menace of private lakes: If you pay a lot to fish and catch nothing, the idea of all that money going to waste forces you to do things you wouldn't do otherwise. That, at least, is what happened to me. Feeling the onset of desperation, I searched deep in my tackle cache and found a small package of adhesive-backed foam strike indicators. The package had never been opened, but I opened it then. Next, using my anchor rope, I measured the depth where I was fishing, tied on a leader tippet long enough to reach within a foot of the bottom, knotted a chironomid imitation to the end of the tippet, pinched one of the adhesive indicators onto the leader butt, and cast the whole arrangement as far as I could. After that I "assumed the position," hunkering down to stare at the floating indicator. Despite the evidence all around me that the method worked, I didn't have much confidence in the result, mainly because I'd never before tried fishing this way.

One thing I discovered early on: If you sit motionless staring at a strike indicator, it doesn't take long for the cold to seep through multiple layers of clothing until you begin to feel it in your bones. I wondered what would happen first: Would the strike indicator disappear under the surface, or would I fall victim to hypothermia?

Suddenly the question was answered: The indicator dipped. I lifted my rod and felt the weight of a heavy fish. Grateful for the opportunity to stand up and move, I played the trout, which fought as well as it could given the frigid temperature. After it was subdued and released, I cast again, and within moments the whole process was repeated. After that I landed two more trout and missed several others before the anemic early winter sun dipped below the horizon and we quit fishing before frostbite could set in.

Those four trout were the most expensive I've ever caught. They also remain the only ones I've ever caught using that particular fishing technique.

Things went a little better when my son and I spent a couple of days fishing a different private water, my birthday gift to him. This was a very scenic lake, occupying a natural rock amphitheater carved by an ice-age flood. It was in the middle of nowhere, so isolated from civilization that a small band of wild horses had adopted it as their watering hole.

We had been told to expect rainbow up to twenty-four inches plus occasional brown trout even larger. What we found were many rainbow from sixteen to twenty inches, but nothing larger. We also caught many fingerling bass. It turned out the lake's owner, in a colossal case of misjudgment, had planted bass in the lake because he thought the trout needed more to eat. What happened instead is what usually happens when bass are stocked on top of an existing trout population; the bass quickly overpopulated and began consuming the lake's natural feed stocks, leaving less for the trout, and that's why the trout's size was decreasing.

We had a good time, but I figured the lake had only two or three years left before it would no longer be worth fishing, unless the owner figured out a way to get rid of the bass.

To my knowledge, neither of the lakes just mentioned ever has been open to the public, but I was invited to fish another that had once been a popular public fishery. I hadn't fished it when it was open to the public but several friends had, and they were bitterly resentful when the lake's owner closed public access and made it a pay fishery. I sympathized with their feelings and thought of refusing the invitation, but finally decided that wouldn't change anything; it would merely deprive me of a day's fishing. So I accepted.

The lake was at a fair elevation in the eastern foothills of the Cascades. Since I had been invited to fish, I had no control over the timing, and the date fixed for my visit seemed awfully early to me. That judgment was confirmed when I arrived at the lake and found patches of snow still visible in shaded areas around the shore. The lake itself also had just completed its spring "turnover," leaving the water murky and full of gunk stirred up from the bottom. No insects were hatching and no fish were rising, and under the circumstances it didn't seem likely we would see either one. The opaque water also made it impossible to see what the bottom was like or gauge the depth, so I started fishing blind.

A small, sheltered bay seemed promising, so I anchored near the mouth and started casting toward shore. I was using a large black fly, thinking it would be visible in the murky water, and after only a few casts I had a hard strike. The fish was a good one, although it didn't jump or run very far, and I was easily able to bring it to hand, slip the barbless hook from its jaw, and watch it disappear back into the murk. I judged its weight at four pounds or more.

All I knew about the pedigree of the rainbow trout in this lake was that, like trout in most private waters, they had come from a commercial hatchery. Their ancestors undoubtedly had once been wild, but after generations in the hatchery most of the wildness had been bred out of them; they no longer fought with the violence or reckless abandon of wild trout. At least, this one hadn't.

Neither did the others I caught that day. None was as large as the first, and some were dark with spawning colors, doubtless suffering sexual frustration from the lack of any spawning stream flowing into the lake.

Around midafternoon I heard a laboring diesel engine and was surprised to see a hatchery truck lumbering up the road to the lake. This, it seemed, was trout-delivery day. The truck backed up to the shore and the driver got out, attached a big transparent plastic sleeve to a valve on the rear of the truck, and placed the sleeve's other end in the lake. He opened the valve, the sleeve filled with water, and suddenly the truck was vomiting two- and three-pound rainbow trout down the sleeve into the lake. I've seen this quite a few times but it's always interesting to watch. It's also a little unsettling, because it's a reminder that you're witnessing the final step in an industrial process. This is not how nature intended lakes should be filled with trout.

But that's mostly what we now have in private waters: domesticated trout for domesticated fishermen.

The wave of the future? Better get used to it.

ON THE WILD SIDE

THE WILD Steelhead Coalition is an organization whose purpose is preservation of wild native runs of steelhead, many now endangered and some, sadly, already extinct. I strongly support the coalition's objectives, so when I was asked to speak at one of its meetings I gladly accepted the invitation.

I enjoyed the meeting, but experience as a guest speaker has taught me it's sometimes difficult to judge how your remarks are being received by the audience, and this was one of those times; I came away unsure if I'd done very well. Several months later, however, I got the answer—an invitation to be the keynote speaker at the coalition's annual general meeting.

On that occasion the audience and I were definitely on the same page, connected by a mutual regard for wild steelhead and a shared commitment to save those remaining. My remarks also eventually reached far beyond the listening audience; the coalition posted them on its website and later they were published in a pair of magazines circulated among fly fishers.

Looking back, I think the words I spoke that evening also might serve as an appropriate and hopeful conclusion to this book.

After all, it began with a fish; it seems only fitting it should end with another.

Here's what I had to say:

It seems only yesterday that I last spoke to this group, although it was actually nine months ago. I want to thank you for inviting me back, and I'm especially glad you invited me to join tonight's celebration of the miracle of wild steelhead.

For that, as I perceive it, is the reason we are here. We come from many different walks of life and a great diversity of backgrounds, but a love for wild steelhead is the one thing we all have in common. It has given us this opportunity to visit with old friends, hear some outrageous fish stories, share a good dinner, try our luck in the raffle, and risk our fortunes in the auction, all to benefit the cause of preserving wild steelhead.

And that's as it should be. But I think there's a bit more going on here than that. The love we all share for wild steelhead is a complex and mysterious thing that defies easy explanation or analysis. After all, what else could compel us to stand for countless hours in cold rivers, often under rain, casting endlessly in the single-minded hope that perhaps the very next cast will result in the thing we most desire: the shock of a heavy strike or the thrilling sight of a graceful rise.

Not very many people understand this. To be charitable about it, most people think we're crazy. And if you're honest about it, you'd probably have to admit there have been times when you thought so yourself. The truth of the matter is that we don't really understand our own behavior very well.

But I don't think insanity is the answer. I think there are some perfectly rational reasons why wild steelhead have such a magnetic hold over us, why they command us to pursue them with dogged devotion even under the very worst of conditions. And those reasons are what I propose to talk about this evening.

Before venturing any opinions of my own, however, I thought it would be prudent to see what others have had to say about this subject, so I began with a review of the literature of steelhead and steelhead fishing. This didn't take very long because, sadly, there aren't many books about steelhead. In fact, if you compare what has been written about steelhead with what has been written about Atlantic salmon, you quickly find a great disparity. Why should there be such a great difference?

Well, one obvious reason is that the history of fishing for Atlantic salmon goes back much further than the history of steelhead fishing. People have been fishing for steelhead only a little more than a hundred years while the roots of Atlantic salmon fishing date back well before the founding of the republic. So the Atlantic salmon fishermen have had a lot more time to write books than we have.

Another reason is that in the early days of steelhead fishing there was great confusion over the difference between steelhead and Pacific salmon, and those who wrote about it often said they were catching salmon when actually they were probably catching steelhead.

But those aren't the only reasons; the angling historian Paul Schullery has offered a couple of other interesting explanations. He notes that "fishing-book publishing was essentially an Eastern industry; publishers knew the Eastern market and rarely showed interest in the Western market. Something like that may be self-perpetuating; fishermen who grow up with no books about their fishing may well not learn to see fishing as a reader's sport."

Another reason, he says, is that "if you look at the . . . biographies of famous pioneer steelheaders . . . you'll notice that a great many of them were blue-collar workers; this was a different social group than the one that gathered along the shores of the exclusive salmon rivers of eastern Canada, and it was a group much less likely to have the leisure and inclination to write books, especially books of gracious, companionable prose."

I think Schullery is probably right in his assessments, which suggest that steelhead fishermen have always occupied a lower rung on the social ladder than East Coast salmon fishermen. But I don't think we have any reason to feel badly about that; on the contrary, our western tradition of public waters has made steelhead fishing available to just about everybody, and ours has become a truly egalitarian sport—which is much more than you can say about Atlantic salmon fishing. If the price we've had to pay for that is fewer books about steelhead fishing, then I still believe we've gotten the better end of the bargain.

But let's take a look at some of those books and see what they say about the appeal of wild steelhead. The short answer is: not much. This is especially true in the early days. Most of the first writers on the sport were preoccupied describing the appearance and habits of steelhead and their legendary fighting qualities. For example, Zane Grey, the famous western novelist, provided this description of the first steelhead he ever saw, captured by another angler on a visit to Deer Creek in 1918:

"It was a strikingly beautiful fish, graceful, symmetrical, powerfully built, with great broad tail and blunt, pugnacious nose. The faint pinkish color, almost a glow, shone from a background of silver and green." The fish weighed only four pounds, but the man who caught it said "you never could have made me believe he didn't weigh twice" as much.

Grey, like most other early writers, seems to have assumed the steelhead's appearance and game qualities were the reasons why people fished for them. Neither he nor they bothered to inquire any further.

In *The Western Angler*, published in 1939, Roderick Haig-Brown provided an even better description of the steelhead, but his focus, too, was mainly on its appearance and habits, not on its emotional appeal to anglers.

Another Canadian writer, Francis C. Whitehouse, praised the fighting qualities of wild steelhead in his 1945 book, *Sport Fishes of Western Canada.* "The steelhead is an instinctive leaper, and on a fly it will put up an amazing performance," he wrote. "The wild rushes, as if to leave the pool downstream, however, are usually 'bluff;' but if [the fish] actually does so, in some of our rivers, it is just too bad!"

For Whitehouse, as for other writers, the fight was the thing, and he didn't offer any other explanation for his regard for steelhead. But a year later, in 1946, Roderick Haig-Brown returned to the scene with his marvelous book, *A River Never Sleeps*, which almost single-handedly made up for all the previous void in steelhead literature. This book gives us more quotable passages about steelhead than I think can be found in all earlier books put together.

Here's one of my favorites: "The steelhead, with the brightness of the sea still on him, is livest of all the river's life. When you have made your cast for him, you are no longer a careless observer. As you mend the cast and work your fly well down to him through the cold water, your whole mind is with it, picturing its drift, guiding its swing, holding it where you know he will lie. And when the shock of his take jars through you to your forearms and you lift the rod to its bend, you know that in a moment the strength of his leaping body will shatter the water to brilliance, however dark the day."

Nobody ever said it better. But even that vivid description begs the question: What is it, besides the way they look and the way they fight, that we love so much about wild steelhead?

John Atherton, better known as Jack, was an artist and angler who published a highly praised book called *The Fly and the Fish* in 1951. Atherton is remembered mostly as an East Coast angler, but he lived for a time on the Pacific Coast and devoted a chapter of his book to steelhead. And he had this to say about them: "It has always seemed to me that the best fish is the one I am fishing for at the time. But if I could invariably have my choice of locality, river and type of fishing, I am inclined to believe that my favorite would be a fresh-run steelhead in a clear, fast stream. For sheer high explosives on the rod they can hardly be surpassed, and if one eventually beaches this streamlined dynamo, it is mainly due to the grace of the good Lord and a strong wrist."

Again, it was the steelhead's fight that impressed Atherton, and he had little to say about the other qualities of steelhead.

Enos Bradner, my old friend and mentor, was usually more concerned with the nuts and bolts of steelhead fishing than he was with the contemplative aspects of the sport. As outdoor editor of the *Seattle Times*, he had to be. But in 1960, when he received a letter from a teenage boy named Tim, asking for advice on how to become a steelhead fly fisherman, Bradner wrote a reply in which he came as close as he ever did to describing what it feels like to fish for wild steelhead. Here's what he said:

"Everything connected with this sport tugs at the heart . . . You get out right at dawn, walking up a gravel bar to the riffle you hope holds a fish. Anticipation builds up as you step into the water and start working out your sinking fly line . . . The river pushes your waders tight against the body as you work chest-deep into the current. You are alone with and become part of the stream.

"But, Tim, you must have a mountain of patience . . . You must be willing to take long hours of fruitless casting. Perhaps days will go by without the slightest nibble. But then, some enchanted morning, or perhaps even at midday, there will come with startling abruptness a jolt that almost jerks the rod out of your hand. Your reel starts screaming as the steelhead streaks downstream faster than any other game fish can swim. You become alive in every fiber of your system, with adrenaline coursing through your arteries.

"If you are lucky, you finally lead the fish into the shallows and onto the gravel. It lies there, a silver form with maybe a touch of red, as fine a trout as ever was created."

I think that passage captures the essence of steelhead fishing as well as anything ever written. But even in this case I believe some of the real reasons we fish for steelhead are left unsaid.

Trey Combs, in his fine book *Steelhead Fly Fishing*, tells of catching a steelhead and asking it: "'Where have you been?' . . . What collaboration of instincts, what fusion of natural forces sends a hundred smolts to sea and returns to me this single adult? Beyond her own good fortune, what special traits for survival has she brought back for the next generation? Her ocean world is alien to me, and she carries few messages hinting of her past. But these have grown into the small understandings that fill me with admiration for her spirit and wandering ways—characteristics at the core of my romance with this gamefish, and why I am jubilant on this dreary winter day." So, perhaps without realizing it, when Combs asked "where," he really came up with an answer that had more to do with "why" he fishes for steelhead.

But again it was Haig-Brown who first really addressed that question squarely, and his answer left us with one of the most familiar quotations in all of angling literature: "I don't know why I fish or why other men fish, except that we like it and it makes us think and feel. But I do know that if it were not for the strong, quick life of rivers, for their sparkle in the sunshine, for the cold grayness of them under rain and the feel of them about my legs as I set my feet hard down on rocks or sand or gravel, I should fish less often. A river is never quite silent; it can never, of its very nature, be quite still; it is never quite the same from one day to the next. It has its own life and its own beauty, and the creatures it nourishes are alive and beautiful also. Perhaps fishing is, for me, only an excuse to be near rivers. If so, I'm glad I thought of it."

That paragraph, I think, goes a long way toward explaining what motivates us as anglers, and we all share Haig-Brown's excuse: Fishing gives us a reason to be near rivers, and we love wild steelhead because they come to us in rivers.

But even as hypnotic and attractive as they are, I don't think rivers are the sole explanation for our passion. If it weren't for wild steelhead, I'm sure we would all spend less time around rivers. There's something more involved here, some other reason why these fish have such a powerful attraction for us. What is it that we find so compelling about them?

Most of the writers I have quoted remarked on the beauty and fighting qualities of wild steelhead, which are obvious things. But there are other things about steelhead, less obvious, that I think appeal to us on a deeper, perhaps even subconscious level. One of them, I believe, is that we intuitively realize steelhead are the most honest and uncompromising creatures we will ever meet, and we can meet them only on their terms. No steelhead has ever been indicted, and I daresay none will ever be. If only we could say as much for the members of our own species.

Yet there's even more to it than that, some other quality about these fish that makes them almost irresistible to us. I have thought deeply about this, trying to figure out the nature of this powerful attraction, and I think for the answer we must ultimately look to ourselves, not to the fish. And if we do that, I think we will find that deep down, at some primal level of our being, we share a powerful emotional link with wild steelhead.

How could this be? How can we, as intelligent, warm-blooded, air-breathing beings, have some sort of deep-seated connection with an instinctive, cold-blooded creature that dwells in a world completely different from our own? The answer is that wild steelhead possess the very qualities we most deeply admire among ourselves: perseverance, courage, and lonely survival against great odds.

Consider: A steelhead born of the river, who lives long enough to escape to the sea, who makes its way a thousand miles or more across the trackless ocean, stalked by predators every inch of the way, who survives to return and find the river of its birth, and who then fights its way upstream against the relentless weight of water that opposes every millimeter of its progress, and who finally spawns and fulfills the purpose of its life—such a creature is a hero, an inspiration, a model for us all. Small wonder that we should admire it so, or seek, even subconsciously, to emulate its virtues. Small wonder that we should marvel at its achievements, especially during a time in our history when wild steelhead are threatened over so much of their native range.

So that, I think, is what really brings us together here tonight: our common devotion to a fish whose virtues we not only admire but wish we shared. And that devotion, I believe, is what drives our efforts to preserve wild steelhead, the noble purpose to which this organization has dedicated itself.

I need not tell you that the task of preservation will be difficult, because we who love wild steelhead represent the very smallest minority of society. We face the hostility of all who would destroy steelhead habitat for personal gain, plus the vast apathy and indifference of the great majority of our fellow citizens, people who have never known the excitement or experienced the emotional voltage of a connection with wild steelhead.

Yet that's no cause for discouragement; instead, we should feel grateful, for we are among the few who have been fortunate enough to catch a wild steelhead, to experience one of life's greatest thrills, one that most people will never know. It would be well to remember that on those occasions when it seems as if all the world is indifferent or opposed to us.

And there will be such occasions. The road ahead will offer defeats as well as victories, and defeat often brings despair. But this organization cannot afford the luxury of despair, because there is only one way the battle to preserve wild steelhead will ever end—and that is if you surrender.

So let the steelhead be your example. When things get tough, when the situation seems hopeless, remember the qualities we most admire about wild steelhead: perseverance, courage, and lonely survival against great odds.

Without such an inspiration, you cannot succeed. With it, you cannot fail.

CREDITS

SOME PORTIONS of this book were published previously or have been adapted from the texts of oral presentations. They are:

"A Seasonal Passion" was first published in slightly different form in *Wild Steelhead & Atlantic Salmon* magazine, Vol. 2, No. 2, summer, 1995.

"The Man from Campbell River" includes portions of *Special Collections,* first published as a "Seasonable Angler" column in *Fly Fisherman* magazine, Vol 39, No. 3, March, 2008, plus an adaptation from the text of an oral presentation to the annual general meeting of the British Columbia Federation of Fly Fishers at the University of Victoria May 26, 2001, subsequently published in *Fly Lines,* a publication of the BCFF, winter, 2004.

"Better than Strawberries" was adapted from the text of an oral presentation to a graduate seminar on ocean resource management at the University of Washington, 1998.

"Chernobyl Tomato" was first published as a "Seasonable Angler" column in *Fly Fisherman* magazine, Vol. 42, No. 5, Aug- Sep, 2011.

"On the Wild Side" is adapted from the text of a speech given at the annual general meeting of the Wild Steelhead Coalition in Seattle,

November 19, 2005, and subsequently published in *The Osprey,* publication of the Steelhead Committee of the International Federation of Fly Fishers, issue No. 54, May 2006, and *The Flyfisher* magazine, Vol. XL, No. 1, winter, 2007.

Two quotations from Roderick Haig-Brown in "On the Wild Side" also appeared earlier in "The Man from Campbell River." This was intentional; the author considers those quotations essential to both selections.